WALKING IN GODLINESS

A Daily Journey Through Proverbs to Reflect God's Character

By Risa Stegall
Shepherd's Word Publishing

I0079318

Scripture quotations are taken from the Holy Bible, New International Version®, NIV®. Copyright ©1973, 1978, 1984, 2011 by Biblica, Inc.® Used by permission. All rights reserved worldwide.

ISBN: 979-8-9988435-1-8

Printed in the United States of America

First Edition

Published by Shepherd's Word Publishing

Dedication

This book is dedicated to the godly women who shaped my life and legacy: my mother, Eddie Mae Stegall (Bonnie); my grandmother, Nettie Burns; and my great-grandmother, James Anna Kendrick. Each of you, now in the presence of the Lord, lived a life of godliness that left a lasting imprint not only on me but on everyone you encountered. Your strength, faith, and unwavering devotion to God molded me into the woman I am today. This is for you—with honor, love, and deep gratitude.

Acknowledgments

To everyone who has prayed, encouraged, or spoken life over this journey, thank you. To my readers, may this book lead you closer to God's heart. And most of all, to my Savior Jesus Christ, the source of every word and every breath. Without You, none of this would exist. May You receive all the glory. In Jesus name, Amen.

Table of Contents

Introduction to Walking in Godliness:

There was a time in my life when I thought I had everything figured out. I was making decisions based on my own understanding, pursuing success as the world defines it, and believing I was on the right path. Yet, despite my achievements, an unshakable longing remained—an inner knowing that there was more to life than what I was experiencing.

One day, as I reflected on my journey, I realized the limitations of my own wisdom. It was then that I turned to the book of Proverbs, seeking guidance from God's Word. Through my study, I began to understand what it truly means to walk in godliness. It isn't merely about knowing the right things to do—it's about surrendering to God's will, aligning my heart with His, and allowing His wisdom to shape my decisions, relationships, and character.

This book is a journey through the principles of Proverbs, exploring how godliness influences our daily lives. Through scripture, reflection, and real-life application, we will uncover how to align ourselves with God's will, cultivate wisdom, build strong relationships, and develop a heart that honors Him in all things. I invite you to walk this path with me as we pursue a life that reflects God's righteousness and purpose.

Chapter 1: The Foundation of Godliness – The Fear of the Lord

Scripture:
"The fear of the Lord is the beginning of wisdom, and the knowledge of the Holy One is understanding." – Proverbs 9:10

Introduction:
The fear of the Lord is not dread, but a deep reverence for God's holiness, power, and authority. It's the foundation of godliness and the root of wisdom. Living in reverence toward God transforms how we speak, act, and think. This fear causes us to humble ourselves and seek His way above our own.

Biblical Example – Solomon:
When Solomon became king, he didn't ask for riches or fame—he asked for wisdom. His request pleased God because it reflected reverence and dependence. As a result, Solomon was granted unmatched wisdom, and his leadership brought peace and prosperity to Israel.

Reflection Questions:

- Do I live each day with reverence for God's holiness?
- In what areas am I relying on my own understanding rather than fearing the Lord?
- How does the fear of God show up in my speech and actions?

Practical Wisdom for Today:

- Begin your day by acknowledging God's sovereignty.
- In each decision, ask: "Does this honor God?"
- Choose humility over pride in conversations and conflicts.

Real-Life Story:
There was a time when I had to choose between a better-paying job and a role that allowed me to serve God's people more directly. I feared losing out financially, but the fear of the Lord led me to choose purpose over paycheck. God honored that choice and provided in ways I couldn't imagine.

Biblical Person Who Did:
Solomon – who revered the Lord and received wisdom beyond measure.

Biblical Person Who Didn't:
Saul – whose disobedience and lack of reverence cost him his kingship.

Key Verses to Reflect On:

- Proverbs 1:7
- Proverbs 14:27
- Psalm 111:10

Prayer:
Lord, help me to walk in reverent fear of You. Teach me to honor You in every thought, word, and action. Let Your holiness shape my heart and Your wisdom direct my path. In Jesus name, Amen.

Call to Action:
This week, reflect on one area of your life where you're not showing reverence to God. Repent and ask for wisdom to honor Him in that area.

Teaching (Part 1):

The foundation of a godly life is built upon the fear of the Lord. It is not fear that drives us away but a reverent awe that draws us near. Proverbs 9:10 tells us, *"The fear of the Lord is the beginning of wisdom."* Without the fear of God, there can be no true wisdom or godliness.

The fear of the Lord keeps us humble, obedient, and mindful of His holiness. It reminds us that He is sovereign and that our lives are accountable to Him. It anchors us, giving us the right perspective on life, decisions, and relationships. In a world that calls us to exalt ourselves, the fear of God calls us to surrender.

Those who fear the Lord walk carefully, speak cautiously, and love deeply. It is the posture of a heart fully submitted to God — and it is the beginning of becoming more like Him.

Teaching (Part 2):

The fear of the Lord is not about being terrified of God — it's about having a profound reverence and awe for who He is. It's the recognition of His holiness, justice, and majesty that leads us to humble submission and obedience. Proverbs 1:7 says, *"The fear of the Lord is the beginning of knowledge, but fools despise wisdom and instruction."*

When we fear the Lord, we acknowledge His authority over our lives. This reverence leads us to live with integrity, humility, and wisdom. The fear of God guards us against sin and draws us closer to His heart. It produces in us a worshipful attitude that permeates every area of our lives — decisions, relationships, and actions.

Without the fear of the Lord, godliness becomes shallow and self-centered. True godliness flows from a heart that honors God above all else, prioritizes His Word, and seeks to live in a way that pleases Him. The fear of the Lord is the foundation — the starting point — upon which a life of true godliness is built.

Reflection Questions:

1. What does the fear of the Lord mean to you personally?

2. How does a reverent fear of God shape the way you live daily?

3. Are there areas in your life where you have lost the awe of God's holiness?

4. In what ways can the fear of the Lord deepen your wisdom and decision making?

5. Write a short prayer asking God to restore or strengthen your fear of Him.

Closing Prayer:

"Heavenly Father, I humble myself before Your majesty. Teach me to walk in reverent fear of You, knowing that it is the beginning of all wisdom. Help me to honor You with my thoughts, words, and actions. May my life reflect Your holiness. In Jesus' name, Amen."

Verses for Meditation:

- **Proverbs 9:10** — *"The fear of the Lord is the beginning of wisdom, and knowledge of the Holy One is understanding."*
- **Psalm 111:10** — *"The fear of the Lord is the beginning of wisdom; all who follow His precepts have good understanding."*
- **Ecclesiastes 12:13** — *"Fear God and keep His commandments, for this is the whole duty of man."*

Key Takeaways:

- Godliness begins with a right view of God — reverence and awe.
- The fear of the Lord produces wisdom and obedience.
- Walking in the fear of the Lord keeps our hearts humble and our lives aligned with His will.

Real-Life Testimony:

John was a young professional pursuing success at any cost. After hearing a sermon on the fear of the Lord, his heart was pierced. He realized that his self-centered ambition left no room for God's direction. That day, John decided to submit his career to God's will, and he saw not only success but a deeper peace and integrity in his work.

Chapter 2: Wisdom – The Path to Godliness

Scripture:
"Wisdom is the principal thing; therefore get wisdom. And in all your getting, get understanding." – Proverbs 4:7

Introduction:
Wisdom is more than knowledge—it's divine insight into how to live. Proverbs teaches us that wisdom protects, promotes, and preserves those who embrace it. Godly wisdom helps us discern the right paths and avoid costly mistakes.

Biblical Example – Solomon:
When Solomon ruled with God's wisdom, he rendered just decisions, such as the famous case with two women claiming the same child. His insight amazed the people and brought glory to God.

Reflection Questions:

- Do I ask God for wisdom before making decisions?
- Am I open to godly counsel?
- How can I pursue wisdom more intentionally?

Practical Wisdom for Today:

- Spend daily time in Proverbs or James.
- Seek wise mentors, not just popular opinions.
- Let the Holy Spirit guide you before reacting emotionally.

Real-Life Story:
There was a time I rushed into a decision without prayer. The outcome was stressful and avoidable. I've learned that slowing down to seek wisdom—through God's Word and godly counsel—saves time, energy, and heartache.

Biblical Person Who Did:
Solomon – chose wisdom above all.
Biblical Person Who Didn't:
Rehoboam – rejected elder counsel and divided the kingdom.

Key Verses:

- James 1:5
- Proverbs 3:13–18
- Proverbs 2:6

Prayer:
Father, I seek Your wisdom today. Help me to walk in understanding and insight, to make decisions that reflect Your will and bring peace. In Jesus name, Amen.

Call to Action:
Before you make any major decision this week, pause and ask God for wisdom. Then seek confirmation in His Word.

Teaching (Part 1):

Wisdom is more than knowledge — it is knowledge rightly applied. In Scripture, wisdom is closely tied to godliness because it teaches us how to live rightly before God and man. Proverbs 4:7 declares, *"Wisdom is the principal thing; therefore get wisdom: and with all thy getting get understanding."*

The path to godliness is not one of self-effort but of divinely given insight. Wisdom allows us to discern God's will and walk in it faithfully. It helps us avoid the traps of pride, deception, and foolishness. Through wisdom, we build lives that honor God and reflect His character.

Teaching (Part 2)

Those who seek wisdom seek the heart of God. James 1:5 reminds us that God gives wisdom generously to those who ask. A life of godliness is impossible without this divine wisdom. It guards our decisions, governs our relationships, and guides our conduct.

Wisdom begins with humility — acknowledging that we do not have all the answers. It flourishes through prayer, meditation on the Word, and obedience. Every godly person in Scripture, from Solomon to Paul, walked in divine wisdom. If we are to live godly lives, wisdom must be our constant companion.

Reflection Questions:

1. What is the difference between wisdom and knowledge in your life?

2. How has godly wisdom shaped your decisions in the past?

3. In what areas are you currently seeking wisdom?

4. Why is humility important in gaining wisdom?

5. Write a prayer asking God for wisdom in a specific area of your life today.

Closing Prayer:

"Lord, I seek Your wisdom, knowing that it is the key to walking in Your ways. Teach me to listen, to learn, and to walk in humility. Let wisdom govern my heart and guide my path. In Jesus' name, Amen."

Verses for Meditation:

- **Proverbs 4:7** — *"Wisdom is the principal thing; therefore get wisdom: and with all thy getting get understanding."*
- **James 1:5** — *"If any of you lacks wisdom, let him ask of God, who gives generously to all without finding fault, and it will be given to him."*
- **Ecclesiastes 7:12** — *"Wisdom preserves those who have it."*

Key Takeaways:

- Wisdom is essential for a life of godliness.
- Wisdom begins with humility and flourishes in obedience.
- God generously gives wisdom to those who ask in faith.

Real-Life Testimony:

Maria struggled for years with major life decisions. She sought advice from friends but often ended up confused and frustrated. When she began to pray specifically for God's wisdom, her life began to change. She made choices with clarity and peace, seeing doors open that aligned with God's timing and provision. Wisdom led her from chaos to calm.

Chapter 3: Humility – The Path to Honor

Scripture:
"Before honor is humility." – Proverbs 15:33

Introduction:
Humility is the soil where godliness grows. It's not thinking less of yourself but thinking of yourself less. God resists the proud but gives grace to the humble.

Biblical Example – Jesus Washing Feet:
Jesus, King of kings, washed His disciples' feet, showing that the greatest among us must be a servant. His humility led to exaltation.

Reflection Questions:

- Do I struggle with pride in my words or decisions?
- How do I respond when corrected?
- In what ways can I serve others this week?

Practical Wisdom:

- Practice listening more than speaking.
- Serve quietly without needing applause.
- Acknowledge God's hand in your success.

Real-Life Story:
I once felt overlooked in a group project and wanted to prove my value. But God reminded me that He sees me even when people don't. I chose to stay humble—and later, others began to recognize my quiet leadership.

Biblical Person Who Did:
Jesus – humbled Himself to serve.
Biblical Person Who Didn't:

Nebuchadnezzar – boasted of his kingdom and was humbled by God.

Key Verses:

- Philippians 2:3–4
- James 4:10
- Proverbs 22:4

Prayer:
Lord, help me walk in humility. Strip away pride and self-importance, and teach me to serve with joy. May others see Your character in my humility. In Jesus name, Amen.

Call to Action:
This week, do something kind for someone without telling them or expecting anything in return.

Teaching (Part 1):

Humility is a rare and precious virtue. In a world that teaches us to exalt ourselves, God calls us to humble ourselves under His mighty hand. Proverbs 22:4 reminds us, *"By humility and the fear of the Lord are riches, honor, and life."* True honor is not grasped by ambition but granted by God to those who walk humbly before Him.

Humility is not weakness — it is strength under control. It is recognizing that all we have and all we are comes from God. It leads us to submit willingly to His will, to serve others without seeking recognition, and to acknowledge that His plans are greater than ours.

18

Teaching (Part 2)

Jesus, our perfect example, humbled Himself even to the point of death on a cross (Philippians 2:8). If the Son of God chose humility, how much more should we? Humility opens the door for God's grace and positions us to receive His blessings. *"God opposes the proud but gives grace to the humble"* (James 4:6).

The path to honor in God's kingdom is not paved with pride but with humility. When we humble ourselves, God lifts us up in due time (1 Peter 5:6). A life of godliness is marked by a heart that bows low before the Lord and serves others with joy.

Reflection Questions:

1. How do you define humility in your own words?

2. What are some areas in your life where pride needs to be replaced with humility?

3. How does humility invite God's grace into your life?

4. What does it mean to follow Jesus' example of humility in your daily actions?

5. Write a prayer asking God to cultivate a humble heart within you.

Closing Prayer:

"Lord, teach me to walk in humility as Jesus did. Help me to submit to Your will and to serve others without seeking recognition. Strip away pride and fill my heart with the beauty of true humility. In Jesus' name, Amen."

Verses for Meditation:

- **Proverbs 22:4** — *"By humility and the fear of the Lord are riches, honor, and life."*
- **James 4:6** — *"God opposes the proud but gives grace to the humble."*
- **1 Peter 5:6** — *"Humble yourselves, therefore, under God's mighty hand, that he may lift you up in due time."*

Key Takeaways:

- Humility is the pathway to true honor in God's kingdom.
- God gives grace to the humble and opposes the proud.
- Following Jesus' example of humility leads to divine promotion.

Real-Life Testimony:

Anthony had achieved much success early in his career, but pride caused him to look down on others. After facing a humbling setback, he surrendered his heart to God and learned the power of humility. Over time, he was restored, promoted, and became a leader known not for arrogance, but for grace and servant-hearted leadership. Humility opened the doors that pride had once closed.

Chapter 4: Integrity – Walking in Truth

Scripture:
"The righteous who walks in his integrity—blessed are his children after him." – Proverbs 20:7

Introduction:
Integrity means being whole living in truth when no one is watching. A godly life is not just public holiness but private honesty. Integrity anchors us in storms and earns trust over time.

Biblical Example – Joseph in Egypt:
Joseph was tempted by Potiphar's wife but chose to honor God in secret. His integrity led to prison—but also to promotion.

Reflection Questions:

- Are there areas in my life where I compromise truth?
- Am I consistent in public and private?
- What legacy of integrity do I want to leave?

Practical Wisdom for Today:

- Say what you mean, and follow through.
- Choose honesty, even when it's inconvenient.
- Confess faults and make things right.

Real-Life Story:
I once had to correct an error at work that no one else noticed. It cost me time, but the decision brought peace. Later, my honesty led to unexpected favor and trust from leadership.

Biblical Person Who Did:
Joseph – maintained integrity under pressure.
Biblical Person Who Didn't:

David (with Bathsheba) – momentarily lost integrity and paid deeply.

Key Verses:

- Proverbs 11:3
- Psalm 15:1–2
- Proverbs 10:9

Prayer:
Lord, help me walk in integrity even when it's hard. Let my words and actions align with truth. Strengthen me to live blamelessly. In Jesus name, Amen.

Call to Action:
Review one area of your life where you've compromised integrity—commit to correcting it this week with God's help.

Teaching (Part 1):

Integrity is living a life that aligns with truth, both publicly and privately. It means being the same person behind closed doors as you are in front of others. Proverbs 10:9 says, *"Whoever walks in integrity walks securely, but whoever takes crooked paths will be found out."*

A godly life is a life of integrity. It is not about perfection but about consistency — consistency in character, in speech, and in action. When we walk in truth, we honor God and build trust with others. Integrity protects us from the traps of deceit and hypocrisy, keeping our hearts clean before God.

Teaching (Part 2)

Jesus lived a life of perfect integrity. He spoke truth, lived truth, and was truth personified. As His followers, we are called to walk in the same way. Our words should match our deeds, and our deeds should match the truth of Scripture.

Integrity also means doing the right thing when no one is watching. It means being honest in small things and faithful in what is unseen. When we live with integrity, we can stand firm against accusation, knowing that our lives are a testament to the truth of God at work in us.

Reflection Questions:

1. How would you define integrity in your life?

2. Are there areas where your private life does not match your public life?

3. Why is integrity important for a believer's witness to others?

4. What steps can you take to strengthen your walk in truth?

5. Write a prayer asking God to build and preserve integrity in your heart.

Closing Prayer:

"Father, help me to walk in truth and integrity in every area of my life. May my words, actions, and heart align with Your will. Strengthen me to be honest in the small things and faithful in the unseen. In Jesus' name, Amen."

Verses for Meditation:

- **Proverbs 10:9** — *"Whoever walks in integrity walks securely, but whoever takes crooked paths will be found out."*
- **Psalm 25:21** — *"May integrity and uprightness protect me, because my hope, Lord, is in you."*
- **Proverbs 11:3** — *"The integrity of the upright guides them, but the unfaithful are destroyed by their duplicity."*

Key Takeaways:

- Integrity is consistency between your public and private life.
- God calls us to walk in truth in all we do.
- Integrity builds trust with others and honor before God.

Real-Life Testimony:

Cynthia worked in a competitive industry where cutting corners was common. She chose to uphold integrity, even when it cost her a promotion. Later, her honesty and reputation opened greater doors — ones no deceit could have earned. Her life became a testimony that honoring God with integrity is always worth it.

Chapter 5: Diligence – Faithful in the Small Things

Scripture:
"The hand of the diligent will rule, but the lazy will be put to forced labor." – Proverbs 12:24

Introduction:
God honors diligence. Working faithfully—even in hidden things—prepares us for leadership. Diligence isn't perfection; it's consistent, wholehearted effort for God's glory.

Biblical Example – Nehemiah Building the Wall:
Despite opposition and threats, Nehemiah stayed focused. His diligence completed a huge project in 52 days because he trusted God and refused to quit.

Reflection Questions:

- Am I procrastinating on something God asked me to do?
- Do I give my best in unseen moments?
- What task is God calling me to finish diligently?

Practical Wisdom:

- Break large goals into small steps.
- Stay faithful in "mundane" tasks.
- Remember who you're really working for—God.

Real-Life Story:
During a long season of behind-the-scenes work, I felt invisible. But God used that time to refine my character. Later, that same diligence opened doors I never expected.

Biblical Person Who Did:
Nehemiah – persistent under pressure.
Biblical Person Who Didn't:
The servant who hid his talent – he wasted what was entrusted.

Key Verses:

- Proverbs 10:4
- Colossians 3:23
- Proverbs 6:6–8

Prayer:
Lord, help me be diligent in what You've placed in my hands. May
I honor You with my time, energy, and focus. In Jesus name,
Amen.

Call to Action:
Pick one task you've delayed. Complete it this week with
diligence, doing it as an offering to God.

Teaching (Part 1):

Diligence is a steady, persistent effort to do what is right, even when no one is watching and the results are not immediate. Proverbs 12:24 tells us, *"Diligent hands will rule, but laziness ends in forced labor."*

God honors those who are faithful in the small things. Jesus taught that *"Whoever can be trusted with very little can also be trusted with much"* (Luke 16:10). A godly life is not built in grand, dramatic moments but in daily, diligent obedience to God's Word.

Diligence requires patience, perseverance, and focus. It's easy to be zealous for a moment, but diligence is zeal that refuses to quit. It is the mark of someone who is not seeking quick results but lasting fruit.

Teaching (Part 2)

When we are diligent with what God has placed in our hands today, He prepares us for greater things tomorrow. Diligence in prayer, diligence in study, diligence in serving others — these daily disciplines build the strong, godly character that God can trust with influence and responsibility.

In a world that celebrates shortcuts and instant success, diligence is a quiet, powerful force that God uses to fulfill His purposes. A diligent life is a godly life because it mirrors the faithfulness of God Himself.

Reflection Questions:

1. What does diligence look like in your daily life?

2. Are there small areas where you've been tempted to neglect faithfulness?

3. How has God used your diligence in the past to bring about growth?

4. Why is being faithful in small things important to God?

5. Write a prayer asking God to strengthen your diligence in both small and large matters.

Closing Prayer:

"Lord, teach me to be diligent in every task You set before me. Help me to be faithful in the small things, trusting that You are shaping my character and preparing me for greater works. Let my diligence reflect Your faithfulness. In Jesus' name, Amen."

Verses for Meditation:

- **Proverbs 12:24** — *"Diligent hands will rule, but laziness ends in forced labor."*
- **Luke 16:10** — *"Whoever can be trusted with very little can also be trusted with much."*
- **Proverbs 13:4** — *"The soul of the sluggard craves and gets nothing, while the soul of the diligent is richly supplied."*

Key Takeaways:

- Diligence is persistent faithfulness in daily life.
- God rewards those who are faithful in small things.
- Diligence builds character and opens doors for greater responsibilities.

Real-Life Testimony:

Marcus started as a janitor in his church, faithfully showing up every week without fanfare. His diligence caught the attention of the leadership, and over time he was entrusted with greater responsibilities. Years later, Marcus became an associate pastor. His life is a testimony that faithfulness in the small things leads to honor in God's time.

Chapter 6: Generosity – Reflecting God's Heart

Scripture:
"The generous soul will be made rich, and he who waters will also be watered himself." – Proverbs 11:25

Introduction:
God is the ultimate Giver. When we give from a place of love and obedience, we reflect His heart. Generosity isn't just about money—it's about time, encouragement, and presence.

Biblical Example – The Widow's Offering:
Jesus noticed a poor widow give two small coins. She gave all she had in faith and trust. Her heart moved heaven more than the wealthy who gave from excess.

Reflection Questions:

- Do I give joyfully and freely, or with conditions?
- Am I generous in both big and small ways?
- What stops me from being more giving?

Practical Wisdom:

- Look for small, consistent ways to give.
- Offer what you have—your time, talents, smile.
- Trust God to supply your needs as you bless others.

Real-Life Story:
One holiday I felt I had little to offer—but I cooked a meal for a neighbor. That simple act turned into a deep friendship and a chance to share Christ.

Biblical Person Who Did:
The widow – gave from her need, not abundance.
Biblical Person Who Didn't:
Ananias & Sapphira – pretended to be generous but held back and lied to God.

Key Verses:

- 2 Corinthians 9:6–7
- Luke 6:38
- Proverbs 19:17

Prayer:
Lord, help me give with a cheerful heart. Let me reflect Your love in how I share with others. In Jesus name, Amen.

Call to Action:
Bless someone anonymously this week—with time, resources, or encouragement.

Teaching (Part 1):

Generosity is a reflection of God's nature. The Bible tells us that *"God so loved the world that He gave"* (John 3:16). His giving was not out of obligation but out of love. As His children, we are called to be generous — with our time, talents, resources, and compassion.

Proverbs 11:25 says, *"A generous person will prosper; whoever refreshes others will be refreshed."* Generosity is not measured by the size of the gift but by the size of the heart behind it. A generous heart honors God and blesses others, creating a ripple effect of kindness and grace.

Teaching (Part 2)

Generosity is an act of trust. It acknowledges that everything we have belongs to God and that He is our true Provider. When we give freely, we reflect God's heart to a world desperately in need of His love. Generosity shifts our focus from ourselves to others, building humility and compassion within us.

Jesus praised the widow who gave two small coins because she gave out of her need, not her abundance (Mark 12:43–44). True godliness is marked by a generous spirit — one that gives joyfully, sacrificially, and willingly.

Reflection Questions:

1. How does generosity reflect the character of God?

2. In what areas of your life can you practice greater generosity?

3. What holds you back from giving freely and joyfully?

4. How does generosity strengthen your faith and dependence on God?

5. Write a prayer asking God to develop a generous heart within you.

Closing Prayer:

"Father, You have been so generous to me, giving me life, grace, and every good thing. Teach me to give as You give — joyfully and without hesitation. Make me a vessel of Your love and compassion to those around me. In Jesus' name, Amen."

Verses for Meditation:

- **Proverbs 11:25** — *"A generous person will prosper; whoever refreshes others will be refreshed."*
- **2 Corinthians 9:7** — *"Each of you should give what you have decided in your heart to give, not reluctantly or under compulsion, for God loves a cheerful giver."*
- **Luke 6:38** — *"Give, and it will be given to you. A good measure, pressed down, shaken together and running over, will be poured into your lap."*

Key Takeaways:

- Generosity reflects the giving nature of God.
- True generosity is not about the amount but the heart behind the giving.
- A generous spirit grows faith and blesses both the giver and receiver.

Real-Life Testimony:

Rachel was struggling financially but felt led to give a small but meaningful donation to a family in need. Despite her own situation, she gave joyfully. Weeks later, Rachel received a promotion at work and unexpected financial blessings. She learned firsthand that you cannot out-give God, and generosity opens the door to His provision.

Chapter 7: Wisdom – The Path to Understanding

Scripture:
"The beginning of wisdom is this: Get wisdom. Though it cost all you have, get understanding." – Proverbs 4:7

Introduction:
Wisdom protects, guides, and preserves. It's not optional—it's essential for godliness. When we seek God's wisdom above all, we grow in peace and discernment.

Biblical Example – Solomon's Prayer:
Solomon could have asked for anything—he chose wisdom. That decision led to a fruitful and peaceful reign.

Reflection Questions:

- Do I pursue wisdom in Scripture or rely on opinions?
- Am I teachable?
- What is one area where I need divine understanding?

Practical Wisdom:

- Read one Proverb daily.
- Ask trusted believers for perspective.
- Value correction—it often brings clarity.

Real-Life Story:
I used to rush into decisions. But when I began seeking wisdom through prayer and Scripture, I made fewer mistakes and felt more peace—even when answers didn't come quickly.

Biblical Person Who Did:
Solomon – revered wisdom above riches.

Biblical Person Who Didn't:
Rehoboam – ignored wise counsel and caused national division.

Key Verses:

- James 1:5
- Proverbs 2:6
- Proverbs 3:13–18

Prayer:
Lord, help me love wisdom and seek understanding. Teach me to value Your perspective over my own. In Jesus name, Amen.

Call to Action:
Pray James 1:5 each morning this week and write down one piece of wisdom God gives you.

Teaching (Part 1):

Wisdom and understanding are inseparable companions on the journey of godliness. Proverbs 4:7 reminds us, *"Wisdom is the principal thing; therefore get wisdom. And in all your getting, get understanding."*

Wisdom gives us insight, but understanding teaches us how to apply it. While knowledge fills the mind, wisdom fills the heart, and understanding directs our steps. In a world full of information, what we desperately need is the discernment to know what is true, what is right, and how to live it out.

Godly wisdom isn't just about making good choices — it's about living with eternal perspective, understanding God's heart, and walking in alignment with His purposes.

Teaching (Part 2)

Understanding deepens our relationship with God and with others. It allows us to see beyond appearances, to discern motives, and to respond in love and truth. James 3:17 describes wisdom from above as pure, peace-loving, considerate, and full of mercy.

The pursuit of wisdom leads to understanding, and both lead to godliness. As we ask God for wisdom and seek understanding through His Word and Spirit, we grow into the mature, Christlike individuals we are called to be. Wisdom is the path — understanding is the light that shows us the way.

Reflection Questions:

1. How would you describe the difference between wisdom and understanding?

2. Why is understanding important for a godly life?

3. In what situations do you most need God's wisdom and understanding?

4. How can you seek wisdom and understanding more intentionally in your daily walk?

5. Write a prayer asking God for wisdom that leads to deeper understanding.

Closing Prayer:

"Father, grant me wisdom from above and give me understanding to walk in Your ways. Teach me to seek Your heart and not lean on my own understanding. Guide me in truth and love, so that my life may reflect Your wisdom. In Jesus' name, Amen."

Verses for Meditation:

- **Proverbs 4:7** — *"Wisdom is the principal thing; therefore get wisdom. And in all your getting, get understanding."*
- **James 3:17** — *"But the wisdom that comes from heaven is first of all pure; then peace-loving, considerate, submissive, full of mercy and good fruit, impartial and sincere."*
- **Proverbs 2:6** — *"For the Lord gives wisdom; from His mouth come knowledge and understanding."*

Key Takeaways:

- Wisdom and understanding are both essential for godliness.
- Understanding helps us apply wisdom in daily life.
- God promises wisdom and understanding to those who seek Him.

Real-Life Testimony:

David struggled with impatience and rushed decisions, often regretting his choices. As he began to pray daily for wisdom and understanding, he noticed a change — he became slower to speak, quicker to listen, and more discerning. Over time, his relationships and decision-making improved dramatically, and he attributed his growth to God's guidance through wisdom and understanding.

Chapter 8: Peace – Living in God's Shalom

Scripture:
"The way of the righteous is like the morning sun, shining ever brighter till the full light of day." – Proverbs 4:18

Introduction:
Peace isn't the absence of conflict—it's the presence of God. In Hebrew, "shalom" means wholeness, harmony, and well-being. Godly peace comes from trusting His sovereignty even when life is uncertain.

Biblical Example – Jesus Calming the Storm:
In the middle of a raging storm, Jesus slept. His peace was rooted in full trust of the Father. When He spoke, the wind and waves obeyed.

Reflection Questions:

- Do I let fear rule my thoughts when life gets hard?
- In what areas do I need to trust God more deeply?
- Am I a peacemaker in my relationships?

Practical Wisdom:

- Begin your day with quiet time and prayer.
- Choose calm over reaction in stressful moments.
- Speak peace over your home, mind, and family.

Real-Life Story:
There was a season when anxiety gripped me. I learned to speak Scripture out loud and surrender control to God. Over time, His peace settled in and replaced my fear.

Biblical Person Who Did:
Jesus – lived in perfect peace and shared it freely.

Biblical Person Who Didn't:
Saul – his jealousy and insecurity led to a tormented spirit and restless leadership.

Key Verses:

- Philippians 4:6–7
- John 14:27
- Proverbs 14:30

Prayer:
Prince of Peace, calm the storms within me. Teach me to walk in trust and not fear. May I carry Your peace wherever I go. In Jesus name, Amen.

Call to Action:
Spend 10 minutes in quiet prayer each morning this week, surrendering anxious thoughts to God.

Teaching (Part 1):

Peace is not merely the absence of conflict — it is the presence of God's wholeness. The Hebrew word *shalom* speaks of completeness, welfare, and harmony with God, others, and ourselves. Isaiah 26:3 promises, *"You will keep in perfect peace those whose minds are steadfast, because they trust in you."*

True peace is a fruit of a life surrendered to God. It is not circumstantial or fragile, but strong and lasting, rooted in the presence and promises of God. Jesus said, *"Peace I leave with you; my peace I give you"* (John 14:27). His peace calms storms within us even when the storms around us rage.

Teaching (Part 2)

Living in God's peace means trusting Him completely — with our future, our relationships, and our daily needs. It is an active, not passive, trust. *Shalom* shapes our decisions and guards our hearts and minds in Christ Jesus (Philippians 4:7).

When we live in God's shalom, we become peacemakers, not peacekeepers. Peacemakers bring God's reconciliation into broken situations. They embody the truth that peace is not just a feeling but a power that transforms lives and circumstances. God calls us to live in peace and extend His peace to the world around us.

Reflection Questions:

1. How do you define peace according to God's Word?

2. What areas of your life are lacking God's shalom?

3. How does trust in God lead to deeper peace?

4. How can you become a peacemaker in your relationships?

5. Write a prayer asking God to fill your heart and mind with His perfect peace.

Closing Prayer:

"Father, I thank You for the gift of Your peace. Help me to trust You fully and to rest in Your promises. Fill my heart with Your shalom, and make me a vessel of peace to others. Let Your peace guard my heart and mind through every trial. In Jesus' name, Amen."

Verses for Meditation:

- **Isaiah 26:3** — *"You will keep in perfect peace those whose minds are steadfast, because they trust in you."*
- **John 14:27** — *"Peace I leave with you; my peace I give you. I do not give to you as the world gives. Do not let your hearts be troubled and do not be afraid."*
- **Philippians 4:7** — *"And the peace of God, which transcends all understanding, will guard your hearts and your minds in Christ Jesus."*

Key Takeaways:

- God's peace (*shalom*) is completeness and wholeness.
- True peace comes from trusting God fully.
- Living in peace empowers us to become peacemakers.

Real-Life Testimony:

After losing his job, Jonathan battled anxiety and fear. As he spent time in prayer and meditation on God's promises of peace, his heart began to settle. Even before he found a new job, he experienced a calm assurance that God was in control. Jonathan's testimony is proof that peace is not found in circumstances but in Christ alone.

Chapter 9: Righteousness – Living by God's Standard

Scripture:
"The path of the righteous is like the morning sun, shining ever brighter till the full light of day." – Proverbs 4:18

Introduction:
Righteousness is right standing with God—and right living before Him. It's not earned, but it's revealed in our obedience. Godly living isn't perfection; it's persistent alignment with His will.

Biblical Example – Daniel in Babylon:
Daniel refused to eat defiled food or stop praying, even when threatened with death. His righteousness led to favor with kings and glory to God.

Reflection Questions:

- Where in my life have, I compromised righteousness for comfort?
- Do I stand for truth even when it costs me?
- How can I grow in consistent obedience?

Practical Wisdom:

- Don't follow the crowd if it leads away from God.
- Set boundaries to protect your purity.
- Keep short accounts with God—confess and return quickly.

Real-Life Story:
I once found myself justifying a friendship that pulled me away from God's standards. After conviction, I let it go. Though painful, my peace returned, and so did clarity.

Biblical Person Who Did:
Daniel – consistent in righteousness under pressure.
Biblical Person Who Didn't:
Lot – compromised his values by staying in Sodom.

Key Verses:

- Matthew 6:33
- Psalm 1:1–3
- Proverbs 10:6

Prayer:
Lord, help me walk in righteousness—not by my strength, but by Your Spirit. Let my life reflect Your purity and truth. In Jesus name, Amen.

Call to Action:
Ask the Holy Spirit to show you any area of compromise. Repent and commit to righteousness in that area.

Teaching (Part 1):

Righteousness is not about human perfection; it is about living according to God's standard. Proverbs 21:3 says, *"To do righteousness and justice is more acceptable to the Lord than sacrifice."* God is not seeking outward rituals — He is looking for inward alignment with His will.

Through Christ, we are made righteous before God (2 Corinthians 5:21). Yet, we are also called to live out that righteousness daily — in our actions, words, and decisions. It means choosing what is right even when it is hard, standing for truth even when it is unpopular, and reflecting God's holiness in a world that often dismisses it.

Teaching (Part 2)

Living by God's standard requires that we seek His Word and allow it to shape our values and behavior. Psalm 1:6 tells us, *"For the Lord watches over the way of the righteous, but the way of the wicked leads to destruction."*

Righteousness brings peace, favor, and stability. It sets a foundation that cannot be shaken. As we walk in righteousness, we testify to the transforming power of God, drawing others not to ourselves, but to Him. A godly life is a righteous life — not by human effort, but by grace through faith, empowered by the Holy Spirit.

Reflection Questions:

1. How do you define righteousness based on God's Word?

2. What is the difference between self-righteousness and godly righteousness?

3. In what areas of your life is God calling you to align more closely with His standards?

4. How does living righteously impact your witness to others?

5. Write a prayer asking God to guide you in living righteously by His power.

Closing Prayer:

"Lord, thank You for clothing me in the righteousness of Christ. Teach me to walk daily in Your truth and to live according to Your standards. Strengthen me to choose what is right even when it's difficult, and let my life glorify You. In Jesus' name, Amen."

Verses for Meditation:

- **Proverbs 21:3** — *"To do righteousness and justice is more acceptable to the Lord than sacrifice."*
- **2 Corinthians 5:21** — *"God made him who had no sin to be sin for us, so that in him we might become the righteousness of God."*
- **Psalm 1:6** — *"For the Lord watches over the way of the righteous, but the way of the wicked leads to destruction."*

Key Takeaways:

- Righteousness is living according to God's standard, not human perfection.
- Christ is our righteousness, and we are called to walk in that righteousness daily.
- A righteous life reflects God's character and draws others to Him.

Real-Life Testimony:

Karen faced pressure at work to compromise her ethics for quick success. Choosing to honor God, she refused to take shortcuts. Though it cost her temporarily, her integrity and righteousness eventually led to a promotion and the respect of her peers. Her life showed that God honors those who walk in righteousness.

Chapter 10: Obedience – The Fruit of Faith

Scripture:
"Whoever gives heed to instruction prospers, and blessed is the one who trusts in the Lord." – Proverbs 16:20

Introduction:
Obedience is the outward expression of inward faith. When we trust God, we follow Him—even when it's hard. True godliness is built on a heart that says "yes" to God consistently.

Biblical Example – Abraham Offering Isaac:
God tested Abraham's faith by asking him to sacrifice Isaac. Abraham obeyed, and God provided a substitute. His obedience unlocked generational blessing.

Reflection Questions:

- What has God asked me to do that I'm hesitating on?
- Do I obey when I don't understand?
- How has obedience led to blessing in the past?

Practical Wisdom:

- Don't wait to feel ready act in faith.
- Obedience often comes before understanding.
- Surround yourself with others who value God's Word.

Real-Life Story:
There was a time I resisted making a career change that God clearly directed. When I finally obeyed, I found joy and purpose I had longed for—but only after surrendering.

Biblical Person Who Did:
Abraham – obeyed fully and immediately.

Biblical Person Who Didn't:
Jonah – ran from God's command and ended up in a storm.

Key Verses:

- Deuteronomy 28:1–2
- John 14:15
- Proverbs 19:16

Prayer:
Father, give me a heart that obeys quickly and fully. Help me trust Your plan more than my comfort. I want to walk in step with You. In Jesus name, Amen.

Call to Action:
Write down one instruction God has given you recently—and take action on it this week.

Teaching (Part 1):

Obedience is the outward expression of an inward faith. Jesus said, *"If you love Me, you will keep My commandments"* (John 14:15). True faith produces obedience — not out of obligation, but out of love and trust.

God doesn't desire empty sacrifices; He desires surrendered hearts that respond in faithful obedience. 1 Samuel 15:22 says, *"To obey is better than sacrifice."* When we obey, we demonstrate our belief that God's ways are higher, wiser, and better than our own. Obedience leads to blessing, peace, and a deeper intimacy with God.

Teaching (Part 2)

Obedience is not always easy. It requires surrender and trust, especially when God's instructions seem contrary to our human logic. Abraham's willingness to sacrifice Isaac and Noah's building of the ark are timeless examples of faith-fueled obedience.

Delayed obedience is disobedience. God calls us to respond promptly and wholeheartedly. James 1:22 reminds us to *"Be doers of the word, and not hearers only."* A life of godliness is built upon consistent obedience — listening to God's voice and doing what He says.

Reflection Questions:

1. How does obedience demonstrate your faith in God?

2. What are some areas where you have struggled with delayed obedience?

3. How can immediate obedience strengthen your walk with God?

4. Why does God value obedience more than outward sacrifices?

5. Write a prayer asking God to help you walk in greater obedience.

Closing Prayer:

"Lord, give me a heart that delights in obeying You. Help me to trust Your voice and respond without hesitation. Teach me that obedience is an act of love and faith. May my life be a reflection of faithful surrender. In Jesus' name, Amen."

Verses for Meditation:

- **John 14:15** — *"If you love Me, you will keep My commandments."*
- **1 Samuel 15:22** — *"To obey is better than sacrifice."*
- **James 1:22** — *"Do not merely listen to the word, and so deceive yourselves. Do what it says."*

Key Takeaways:

- Obedience is the evidence of true faith and love for God.
- God desires obedience over outward rituals and sacrifices.
- Prompt, wholehearted obedience deepens intimacy with God and brings blessing.

Real-Life Testimony:

Lisa sensed God prompting her to forgive someone who had deeply hurt her, but she resisted. After months of inner turmoil, she finally obeyed. The freedom and peace that followed were immediate. Through her obedience, not only was her heart healed, but her relationship with God deepened significantly.

Chapter 11: Faithfulness – Steadfast in Every Season

Scripture:
"A faithful man will abound with blessings, but he who hastens to be rich will not go unpunished." – Proverbs 28:20

Introduction:
Faithfulness is not about perfection; it is about consistency. God values those who remain steady in their devotion, obedient in their walk, and loyal in their commitments, regardless of the season. Faithfulness reflects the heart of God—who is always faithful to us.

Biblical Example – Ruth's Loyalty to Naomi:
Ruth's life is a beautiful picture of faithfulness. After the death of her husband, she chose to stay with her mother-in-law Naomi rather than return to her homeland. Her words, "Where you go, I will go," revealed a heart committed not just to Naomi, but to Naomi's God. (Ruth 1:16–17) Her faithfulness led her to Boaz and into the lineage of Jesus.

Reflection Questions:
- Am I faithful in the responsibilities God has entrusted to me?
- How do I respond when my faith is tested or I feel overlooked?
- In what areas do I need to remain steadfast even when results are delayed?

Practical Wisdom for Today:
- Show up consistently even when you feel unseen.
- Keep your word—let your 'yes' be yes.
- Trust God's timing, not your own results.

Real-Life Story:
There were seasons in my life when I felt like nothing was
changing. I was doing what God asked—praying, serving,
working—but I saw little progress. Yet as I stayed faithful, God
opened doors I never imagined. Sometimes the fruit of faithfulness
takes time to appear, but it always comes.

Biblical Person Who Did:
Ruth – remained loyal and faithful, resulting in God's reward.

Biblical Person Who Didn't:
King Saul – started with promise, but his unfaithfulness to God's
commands led to his downfall. (1 Samuel 15:22–23)

Key Verses to Reflect On:
- Lamentations 3:22–23 – "Great is Your faithfulness."
- Galatians 6:9 – "Let us not grow weary in doing good…"
- Matthew 25:21 – "Well done, good and faithful servant…"

Prayer:
Lord, help me to be faithful in every season of life. Teach me to
remain steadfast even when the fruit is delayed. Let my heart
mirror Yours in loyalty and endurance. In Jesus name, Amen.

Call to Action:
Stay committed to one task, relationship, or area of responsibility
this week—even if it feels mundane. Let your consistency honor
God.

Teaching (Part 1):

Faithfulness is a rare jewel — the unwavering commitment to remain loyal and consistent no matter the season. Proverbs 3:3–4 says, *"Let love and faithfulness never leave you; bind them around your neck, write them on the tablet of your heart. Then you will win favor and a good name in the sight of God and man."*

Faithfulness is not tested during the easy times but proven during the hard seasons. It's the ability to stay committed to God, to your calling, and to others when it would be easier to walk away. A godly life is a faithful life — showing up, serving, and standing firm even when feelings waver and results are slow.

Teaching (Part 2)

God is the ultimate model of faithfulness — *"His mercies are new every morning; great is Your faithfulness"* (Lamentations 3:23). As His children, we are called to mirror that same steadfastness.

Faithfulness requires trust, perseverance, and a long view. It's sowing seeds consistently, knowing the harvest may take time. It's staying true to your promises, maintaining integrity, and enduring hardship without compromising your values. In every season — in drought and in abundance — the faithful endure, and God honors them.

Reflection Questions:

1. What does faithfulness mean in your relationship with God?

2. How can you remain steadfast when life becomes difficult?

3. In what areas do you need to grow in consistency and loyalty?

4. How does God's faithfulness encourage you to stay faithful?

5. Write a prayer asking God to help you remain faithful through every season.

Closing Prayer:

"Lord, You are faithful beyond measure. Teach me to reflect Your steadfast love and loyalty in my life. Help me to stay faithful in every season — in trials, in waiting, and in joy. Strengthen me to honor You with unwavering commitment. In Jesus' name, Amen."

Verses for Meditation:

- **Proverbs 3:3–4** — *"Let love and faithfulness never leave you; bind them around your neck, write them on the tablet of your heart. Then you will win favor and a good name in the sight of God and man."*
- **Lamentations 3:23** — *"They are new every morning; great is your faithfulness."*
- **1 Corinthians 4:2** — *"Now it is required that those who have been given a trust must prove faithful."*

Key Takeaways:

- Faithfulness is loyalty and consistency, especially in hard seasons.
- God models perfect faithfulness and calls us to reflect it.
- Remaining steadfast honors God and leads to lasting fruit.

Real-Life Testimony:

After many years of ministry, Pastor Thomas saw little visible fruit. Many would have given up, but he remained faithful. Over time, the seeds he planted began to grow — not only in numbers but in deep, transformed lives. His steady faithfulness became a testimony that God honors perseverance.

Chapter 12: Discernment – Recognizing God's Voice

Scripture:
"The heart of the discerning acquires knowledge, for the ears of the wise seek it out." – Proverbs 18:15

Introduction:
Discernment is the spiritual ability to distinguish truth from error, right from wrong, and God's voice from all others. In a world filled with conflicting messages, temptations, and spiritual confusion, discernment keeps us anchored in truth. It is the compass that helps us navigate our faith walk with clarity and wisdom.

Biblical Example – Samuel Hearing God's Voice:
When Samuel was a young boy, he heard a voice calling him at night. At first, he thought it was Eli, but eventually, Eli realized it was God. Samuel responded, "Speak, Lord, for Your servant is listening." (1 Samuel 3:1–10) Samuel's heart posture of listening and obedience made him one of Israel's greatest prophets.

Reflection Questions:
- Do I take time to listen for God's voice, or am I constantly surrounded by noise?
- How can I grow in discerning between God's direction and my own desires?
- Am I seeking truth, even when it challenges my current beliefs or plans?

Practical Wisdom for Today:
- Slow down and seek quiet time daily to listen for God.
- Compare every voice and message to Scripture—God never contradicts His Word.

- Ask the Holy Spirit to sharpen your discernment and give you peace about His direction.

Real-Life Story:
There was a time I faced two good opportunities but didn't know which to pursue. I prayed, fasted, and asked for confirmation. Through Scripture and wise counsel, God gave clarity. The path He confirmed wasn't the most popular, but it was peaceful. Choosing it led to incredible growth and fruit.

Biblical Person Who Did:
Samuel – recognized God's voice early and obeyed it faithfully.

Biblical Person Who Didn't:
Eve – was deceived by the serpent and didn't discern the enemy's voice, leading to the fall. (Genesis 3:1–6)

Key Verses to Reflect On:
- Hebrews 5:14 – "But solid food is for the mature, who by constant use have trained themselves to distinguish good from evil."
- James 1:5 – "If any of you lacks wisdom, let him ask of God..."
- John 10:27 – "My sheep hear My voice, and I know them, and they follow Me."

Prayer:
Father, teach me to hear Your voice above all others. Quiet the distractions and give me discernment rooted in truth. Let my decisions reflect Your wisdom and draw me closer to Your heart. In Jesus name, Amen.

Call to Action:
Practice listening today. Spend five minutes in complete silence before God. Ask Him to speak, and write down what you sense He is saying.

Teaching (Part 1):

Discernment is the ability to distinguish truth from error, light from darkness, and God's voice from all others. Hebrews 5:14 says, *"But solid food is for the mature, who by constant use have trained themselves to distinguish good from evil."*

In a world full of noise and distraction, discernment is essential for a godly life. It keeps us aligned with God's will and guards us from deception. Discernment isn't about suspicion — it's about spiritual sensitivity. It's knowing when to move and when to wait, when to speak and when to remain silent, based not on human reasoning but on divine prompting.

Teaching (Part 2)

God desires to guide us. Jesus said, *"My sheep listen to My voice; I know them, and they follow Me"* (John 10:27). Discernment grows as we spend time in prayer, in the Word, and in obedience. The more intimately we know God, the more clearly we recognize His voice.

Discernment is also critical in relationships, decisions, and ministry. Without it, we can be easily misled or make choices that seem right but lead away from God's best. A discerning heart is anchored in truth and tuned to the whispers of the Holy Spirit.

Reflection Questions:

1. How do you recognize the voice of God in your life?

2. What practices help you grow in discernment?

3. Are there areas where you need greater spiritual discernment right now?

4. How does discernment protect and guide you in your walk with God?

5. Write a prayer asking God to sharpen your spiritual discernment.

Closing Prayer:

"Lord, teach me to hear Your voice above all others. Sharpen my spiritual discernment so that I may walk in truth and avoid the snares of the enemy. Help me to know Your heart intimately and follow Your leading with courage. In Jesus' name, Amen."

Verses for Meditation:

- **Hebrews 5:14** — *"But solid food is for the mature, who by constant use have trained themselves to distinguish good from evil."*
- **John 10:27** — *"My sheep listen to My voice; I know them, and they follow Me."*
- **Proverbs 3:6** — *"In all your ways acknowledge Him, and He will make your paths straight."*

- Discernment is spiritual sensitivity to God's voice and truth.
- It grows through intimacy with God and obedience to His Word.
- A discerning heart is protected from deception and guided into God's best.

Real-Life Testimony:

Maya faced a career decision that looked good on the surface but left her spirit unsettled. Through prayer and time in the Word, she discerned it wasn't God's will. Trusting His leading, she declined the offer. Months later, a better opportunity came — one that aligned perfectly with her calling. Her story shows the blessing of heeding God's voice through discernment.

Chapter 13: Self-Control – Mastering the Flesh

Scripture:
"Whoever has no rule over his own spirit is like a city broken down, without walls." – Proverbs 25:28

Introduction:
Self-control is a fruit of the Spirit and a reflection of God's power working within us. It enables us to resist temptation, make wise choices, and live with purpose. Without self-control, we are vulnerable to every desire, distraction, or emotion. With it, we protect our hearts, honor God, and walk in victory.

Biblical Example – Jesus in the Wilderness:
After His baptism, Jesus fasted for forty days and was tempted by Satan (Matthew 4:1–11). He responded with Scripture and refused to give in. His example shows that victory over temptation begins with self-control, rooted in knowing and obeying God's Word.

Reflection Questions:
- What areas of my life feel out of control or undisciplined?
- How do I respond when I'm tempted or emotionally triggered?
- How can I practice more self-control with my time, words, or habits?

Practical Wisdom for Today:
- Avoid triggers that stir up temptation.
- Replace bad habits with spiritual disciplines like prayer, fasting, or accountability.
- Ask the Holy Spirit for strength before reacting.

Real-Life Story:
There was a time when I struggled with overcommitting. I felt the pressure to say 'yes' to everything, even when it wore me down.

But God began teaching me boundaries. By exercising self-control, I learned to say 'no' with grace and prioritize what truly matters. Peace followed my obedience.

Biblical Person Who Did:
Jesus – maintained perfect self-control in every situation, even under intense pressure.

Biblical Person Who Didn't:
Samson – though chosen by God, often lacked self-control, which led to personal downfall. (Judges 13–16)

Key Verses to Reflect On:
- Galatians 5:22–23 – "But the fruit of the Spirit is… self-control."
- 1 Corinthians 9:27 – "I discipline my body and bring it into subjection…"
- Titus 2:11–12 – "The grace of God teaches us to say 'no' to ungodliness."

Prayer:
Lord, help me to walk in self-control. Strengthen me to resist temptation and to act with wisdom, not impulse. Let my life reflect discipline and devotion to You. In Jesus name, Amen.

Call to Action:
Identify one habit where you need more self-control. Set a boundary or plan, and ask a trusted friend to pray and hold you accountable.

Teaching (Part 1):

Self-control is a hallmark of spiritual maturity. Proverbs 25:28 warns, *"Like a city whose walls are broken through is a person who lacks self-control."* Without self-control, our lives are vulnerable to the attacks of temptation, anger, impulsivity, and pride.

The flesh — our old sinful nature — continually battles against the Spirit. Galatians 5:17 explains, *"For the flesh desires what is contrary to the Spirit, and the Spirit what is contrary to the flesh."* Without discipline, we are easily led astray by emotions, desires, and circumstances.

Self-control is not merely behavior management; it is heart transformation empowered by the Holy Spirit. It enables us to say "no" to sin and "yes" to righteousness. A godly life requires mastering the flesh — not by willpower alone, but by surrendering daily to the Spirit's leading.

Teaching (Part 2):

Self-control is a fruit of the Spirit (Galatians 5:22–23). It cannot be manufactured through human strength; it must be cultivated through relationship with Christ. Titus 2:11–12 teaches that *"the grace of God... teaches us to say 'No' to ungodliness and worldly passions, and to live self-controlled, upright and godly lives in this present age."*

Practicing self-control affects every area: our speech, our appetites, our spending, our time, and our relationships. It is the discipline of bringing every thought captive to Christ (2 Corinthians 10:5), refusing to let our emotions or fleshly desires dictate our behavior.

When we walk in self-control, we protect the calling God has placed on our lives. Mastering the flesh is not about legalism or perfection — it's about freedom. As Paul said, *"I discipline my body and keep it under control, lest after preaching to others I myself should be disqualified"* (1 Corinthians 9:27). Self-control leads to greater freedom, victory, and spiritual authority.

Reflection Questions:

1. How does Scripture describe self-control as a fruit of the Spirit?

2. In what areas do you struggle most with mastering the flesh?

3. How does self-control protect and preserve your spiritual life and calling?

4. What spiritual disciplines can you practice to strengthen self-control daily?

5. Write a prayer asking God to empower you by His Spirit to live a disciplined life.

Closing Prayer:

"Lord, I recognize that without You I am powerless against the desires of the flesh. Teach me to walk in step with Your Spirit and to cultivate true self-control. Strengthen me to live a life of discipline and freedom that honors You. Master my heart, my mind, and my body for Your glory. In Jesus' name, Amen."

Verses for Meditation:

- **Proverbs 25:28** — *"Like a city whose walls are broken through is a person who lacks self-control."*
- **Galatians 5:22–23** — *"But the fruit of the Spirit is love, joy, peace, forbearance, kindness, goodness, faithfulness, gentleness and self-control."*
- **Titus 2:12** — *"It teaches us to say 'No' to ungodliness and worldly passions, and to live self-controlled, upright and godly lives in this present age."*
- **1 Corinthians 9:27** — *"I discipline my body and keep it under control, lest after preaching to others I myself should be disqualified."*
- **2 Corinthians 10:5** — *"We take captive every thought to make it obedient to Christ."*

Key Takeaways:

- Self-control is a supernatural fruit of the Spirit that empowers us to resist sin.
- Mastering the flesh leads to freedom, not bondage.
- Discipline in thought, word, and action protects the calling and purpose God has for your life.

Real-Life Testimony:

David had battled with anger for years. Quick to lash out, he damaged relationships and wounded his own soul. After committing to prayer, Scripture study, and surrender to the Holy Spirit, David gradually saw transformation. He learned to pause, pray, and respond with grace. Self-control not only changed his responses but also restored his relationships and deepened his testimony. His life now reflects the power of a heart mastered by the Spirit rather than the flesh.

Chapter 14: Contentment – Resting in God's Provision

Scripture:
"Better a little with the fear of the Lord than great wealth with turmoil." – Proverbs 15:16

Introduction:
Contentment is the quiet confidence that God's provision is enough. It's not complacency, it's peace rooted in trust. In a world driven by comparison and accumulation, contentment stands out as a powerful testimony that God is our source. When we rest in His provision, we find joy that cannot be taken by circumstances.

Biblical Example – Paul's Contentment in All Circumstances:
In Philippians 4:11–13, Paul declared that he learned the secret of being content whether in plenty or in want. His strength came from Christ, not from possessions or situations. Whether he was imprisoned or free, Paul chose to trust that God would supply all his needs.

Reflection Questions:
- Do I find myself constantly wanting more, or do I thank God for what I have?
- In what ways have I let comparison steal my joy?
- How can I cultivate gratitude for God's daily provision?

Practical Wisdom for Today:
- Start a gratitude journal to reflect on God's daily blessings.
- Limit time on social media to reduce comparison.
- Practice generosity to shift focus from getting to giving.

Real-Life Story:
There was a season when I had little income and mounting responsibilities. Instead of panicking, I chose to praise God for each small provision—a gas card, a kind word, a meal. Those moments reminded me that God sees and supplies. That season didn't change overnight, but my heart did. Contentment grew stronger than my needs.

Biblical Person Who Did:
Paul – learned to be content through every circumstance, trusting Christ's strength.

Biblical Person Who Didn't:
The Israelites in the wilderness – constantly complained despite God's miraculous provision, missing out on deeper blessings. (Numbers 11)

Key Verses to Reflect On:
- 1 Timothy 6:6 – "Godliness with contentment is great gain."
- Hebrews 13:5 – "Be content with what you have, because God has said, 'Never will I leave you.'"
- Philippians 4:11–13 – "I have learned the secret of being content in any and every situation..."

Prayer:
Father, teach me to rest in Your provision. Silence the voices that push me toward comparison and greed. Let my heart be filled with gratitude and peace. May I find my joy in You alone. In Jesus name, Amen.

Call to Action:
Each evening this week, write down three things you're grateful for. Begin training your heart to see and celebrate what God has already given.

Teaching (Part 1):

Contentment is a heart at rest — trusting that God's provision is enough. 1 Timothy 6:6 says, *"But godliness with contentment is great gain."* The world encourages constant striving, comparison, and dissatisfaction, but God calls us to a life of quiet confidence in His goodness.

True contentment isn't based on external circumstances — it's rooted in a relationship with a faithful God. Paul wrote from a prison cell that he had learned the secret of being content in every situation (Philippians 4:11–12). Contentment is not complacency — it is peace that comes from knowing that in God, we lack nothing essential.

Teaching (Part 2)

Resting in God's provision requires us to shift our focus from what we don't have to what we have been given — His grace, His presence, His promises. Contentment grows as we trust that God's timing, gifts, and plans are perfect.

Discontentment robs us of peace and blinds us to God's blessings. Contentment fuels gratitude, strengthens faith, and honors God. A content heart says, "Lord, You are enough for me," regardless of changing seasons. In a godly life, contentment is a powerful testimony of trust in God's unchanging care.

Reflection Questions:

1. How would you describe contentment in your own words?

2. What are the dangers of living with discontentment?

3. How can you practice resting in God's provision daily?

4. In what areas is God inviting you to be more content right now?

5. Write a prayer asking God to cultivate contentment in your heart.

Closing Prayer:

"Father, You are my Shepherd, and I lack nothing. Teach me to rest in Your provision and to trust in Your goodness. Free my heart from striving and comparison. Fill me with the peace of contentment and the joy of Your sufficiency. In Jesus' name, Amen."

Verses for Meditation:

- **1 Timothy 6:6** — *"But godliness with contentment is great gain."*
- **Philippians 4:11–12** — *"I have learned the secret of being content in any and every situation."*
- **Psalm 23:1** — *"The Lord is my shepherd; I shall not want."*

Key Takeaways:

- Contentment is trusting God's provision is enough.
- It produces peace, gratitude, and deepens faith.
- A content heart reflects trust in God's perfect care and timing.

Real-Life Testimony:

Amanda spent years chasing success, always feeling empty no matter how much she achieved. When she surrendered her ambitions to God and chose to rest in His provision, she found the peace and joy that had eluded her. Amanda's life became a testimony that true fulfillment comes not from striving, but from resting in God's sufficiency.

Chapter 15: Patience – Waiting on God's Timing

Scripture:
"A man's heart plans his way, but the Lord directs his steps." –
Proverbs 16:9

Introduction:
Patience is more than waiting—it's trusting God in the waiting. In
a fast-paced world, waiting feels like weakness. But in God's
kingdom, patience is a strength. It demonstrates faith, maturity,
and surrender to His perfect timing. When we trust God's process,
He works behind the scenes in ways we can't yet see.

**Biblical Example – Joseph's Journey from the Pit to the
Palace:**
Joseph was sold by his brothers, falsely accused, and imprisoned—
all before God elevated him to second-in-command in Egypt.
Years passed between promise and promotion, but Joseph
remained faithful. His patience brought about not only personal
breakthrough but salvation for an entire nation. (Genesis 37–41)

Reflection Questions:
- Am I willing to wait for God's best, or am I rushing ahead?
- What is God trying to teach me during this season of waiting?
- Do I believe that God's timing is always better than my own?

Practical Wisdom for Today:
- Use waiting seasons to grow in prayer, character, and obedience.
- Avoid comparison—it steals peace and breeds impatience.
- Remind yourself that God sees the full picture, even when you
don't.

Real-Life Story:
I once prayed for an open door in the ministry, but nothing seemed to happen. For over a year, I served quietly behind the scenes. Looking back, I now see that season as preparation. When God opened the door, I was more ready than I knew. Patience wasn't delayed; it was divine setup.

Biblical Person Who Did:
Joseph – endured betrayal and imprisonment while waiting for God's promise to be fulfilled.

Biblical Person Who Didn't:
King Saul – couldn't wait for Samuel and offered an unlawful sacrifice, leading to his rejection. (1 Samuel 13:8–14)

Key Verses to Reflect On:
- Isaiah 40:31 – "But those who wait on the Lord shall renew their strength…"
- Psalm 27:14 – "Wait for the Lord; be strong and take heart…"
- Galatians 6:9 – "Let us not become weary in doing good…"

Prayer:
Father, teach me to wait well. Help me to trust Your timing and not rush ahead of Your plan. Grow my faith in the delay and prepare me for the blessings You are working on. In Jesus name, Amen.

Call to Action:
Choose one area where you feel rushed. Release it to God in prayer and commit to waiting patiently this week, trusting His timing.

Teaching (Part 1):

Patience is more than passive waiting — it's active trust in God's perfect timing. Psalm 27:14 exhorts us, *"Wait for the Lord; be strong and take heart and wait for the Lord."* Patience teaches us that God's delays are not His denials. His timing is not only perfect but purposeful.

Waiting on God molds our character. It strengthens our faith, builds perseverance, and deepens our dependence on Him. Through patience, we acknowledge that God sees the whole picture, while we only see a part. He is never late, though He rarely moves according to our schedule.

Teaching (Part 2)

Impatience can lead us to make hasty decisions and step outside of God's will. Many in Scripture, like Abraham and Sarah, learned hard lessons about trying to force God's hand. But those who wait upon the Lord renew their strength (Isaiah 40:31).

Patience is a mark of godliness because it reflects trust in God's character. It says, *"I believe You know what's best for me, even if I don't see it yet."* Waiting becomes a form of worship when we rest in the assurance that God is working behind the scenes for our good and His glory.

Reflection Questions:

1. How do you define patience in your walk with God?

2. What challenges do you face when waiting on God's timing?

3. How can patience deepen your faith and trust in God?

4. In what current situation is God asking you to wait and trust Him?

5. Write a prayer asking God to strengthen your patience and trust.

Closing Prayer:

"Lord, help me to wait on You with faith and courage. Teach me to trust Your perfect timing and to rest in Your promises. Let patience have its perfect work in my life, shaping me into the person You've called me to be. In Jesus' name, Amen."

Verses for Meditation:

- **Psalm 27:14** — *"Wait for the Lord; be strong and take heart and wait for the Lord."*
- **Isaiah 40:31** — *"But those who hope in the Lord will renew their strength."*
- **James 5:7–8** — *"Be patient, then, brothers and sisters, until the Lord's coming."*

Key Takeaways:

- Patience is active trust in God's timing and plan.
- Waiting strengthens faith, character, and dependence on God.
- God's timing is perfect — patience aligns us with His will.

Real-Life Testimony:

Daniel waited years for a breakthrough in his career. Tempted to give up many times, he chose instead to trust God's timing. When the door finally opened, it was beyond anything he had imagined — not just a job, but a calling. His story reminds us that God's timing is always worth the wait.

Chapter 16: Kindness – The Strength of a Gentle Spirit

Scripture:
"What is desired in a man is kindness, and a poor man is better than a liar." – Proverbs 19:22

Introduction:
Kindness isn't weakness, it's strength under control. It reflects the character of Christ and has the power to transform hearts. True kindness flows from a heart that's been changed by God's love.

Biblical Example:
The Good Samaritan saw a wounded man and acted with compassion when others passed by. His kindness crossed cultural boundaries and reflected God's heart. (Luke 10:25–37)

Reflection Questions:
- How do I respond to people who are different from me?
- When was the last time I showed kindness without expecting anything in return?
- In what way can I be more intentionally kind this week?

Practical Wisdom for Today:
- Slow down and notice the needs around you.
- Speak words of encouragement daily.
- Let kindness guide your actions, especially in conflict.

Real-Life Story:
There was a day when a coworker came in visibly distressed. I felt prompted to check in, and that small act of kindness opened the door for healing and a deeper friendship.

Biblical Person Who Did:
The Good Samaritan – helped without hesitation.

Biblical Person Who Didn't:
The priest and Levite – passed by the hurting man without compassion.

Key Verses to Reflect On:
- Ephesians 4:32
- Galatians 5:22
- Proverbs 31:26

Prayer:
Lord, clothe me in kindness. Help me to see others through Your eyes and extend grace, even when it's hard. Let my words and actions reflect Your compassion. In Jesus name, Amen.

Call to Action:
Do one act of unexpected kindness today expecting nothing in return.

Teaching (Part 1):

Kindness is often mistaken for weakness, but in God's Kingdom, kindness is a powerful force. Proverbs 11:17 says, *"Those who are kind benefit themselves, but the cruel bring ruin on themselves."* Kindness is not simply being nice — it is the intentional choice to reflect the love and gentleness of Christ in every interaction.

Jesus embodied kindness, welcoming the outcast, healing the broken, and extending grace where others offered judgment. His kindness was never weakness — it was strength under control, rooted in deep compassion and divine authority. A gentle spirit is not fragile but resilient, able to show kindness even when met with hostility.

Teaching (Part 2)

Kindness softens hearts and opens doors to truth. It disarms anger, bridges divides, and carries the fragrance of Christ wherever it goes. Colossians 3:12 instructs us to *"clothe yourselves with compassion, kindness, humility, gentleness, and patience."*

As followers of Christ, kindness should mark our lives — in our homes, workplaces, and communities. It's easy to be kind when treated well, but godly kindness is best demonstrated when it is undeserved. A godly life shines brightest when kindness flows from a heart transformed by the love of God.

Reflection Questions:

1. How do you define kindness according to Scripture?

2. What does it look like to have a gentle spirit in difficult situations?

3. How can you practice kindness even when it's not returned?

4. Why is kindness considered a strength and not a weakness?

5. Write a prayer asking God to cultivate a spirit of kindness and gentleness in you.

Closing Prayer:

"Lord, clothe me in kindness and gentleness. Teach me to reflect Your love in every word and action. Give me strength to respond with grace, even when it is hard. Let my life be a testimony of the powerful kindness found in You. In Jesus' name, Amen."

Verses for Meditation:

- **Proverbs 11:17** — *"Those who are kind benefit themselves, but the cruel bring ruin on themselves."*
- **Colossians 3:12** — *"Clothe yourselves with compassion, kindness, humility, gentleness, and patience."*
- **Ephesians 4:32** — *"Be kind and compassionate to one another, forgiving each other, just as in Christ God forgave you."*

Key Takeaways:

- Kindness is strength wrapped in gentleness, reflecting Christ's heart.
- True kindness is intentional, courageous, and enduring.
- A gentle spirit impacts the world more powerfully than force or anger.

Real-Life Testimony:

Jeremy worked in a tense, competitive office where kindness was rare. He made it his mission to be consistently kind, even to those who were rude. Over time, his attitude softened the environment, and he became a trusted leader. His kindness wasn't weakness — it was the strength that changed the culture around him.

Chapter 17: Joy – Finding Strength in God's Presence

Scripture:
"A merry heart does good, like medicine, but a broken spirit dries the bones." – Proverbs 17:22

Introduction:
Joy isn't the absence of problems—it's the presence of God. It's not a fleeting emotion, but a deep, spiritual strength. Joy renews us and shines as a witness to others.

Biblical Example:
David danced before the Lord with all his might as the Ark of the Covenant returned to Jerusalem. His joy was unashamed and rooted in God's presence. (2 Samuel 6:14–15)

Reflection Questions:
- What robs me of joy?
- Do I seek joy in God or in circumstances?
- How can I choose joy even in hard times?

Practical Wisdom for Today:
- Practice gratitude.
- Worship daily, even in struggle.
- Surround yourself with joy-filled people.

Real-Life Story:
In a season of loss, I felt numb. But as I focused on God's faithfulness and prayer, joy quietly returned and gave me strength to move forward.

Biblical Person Who Did:
David – expressed joy in worship and battle.

Biblical Person Who Didn't:

Michal – despised David's joyful praise and was left barren.

Key Verses to Reflect On:
- Nehemiah 8:10
- Psalm 16:11
- John 15:11

Prayer:

God, restore to me the joy of Your salvation. Let joy be my strength, even in adversity. I choose to rejoice in You. In Jesus name, Amen.

Call to Action:

Each morning this week, declare one reason you have joy in God—out loud.

Teaching (Part 1):

Joy is more than happiness — it is a deep, abiding strength rooted in God's presence. Nehemiah 8:10 proclaims, *"The joy of the Lord is your strength."* Unlike happiness, which depends on circumstances, joy is the unshakable confidence that God is good, God is in control, and God is with us.

Joy sustains us through trials. It empowers us to praise even in pain, to hope even in hardship. In His presence, there is fullness of joy (Psalm 16:11). As we draw near to God, His joy fills the empty and broken places within us, renewing our strength and lifting our spirits.

True joy is not manufactured by positive thinking; it is produced by the Holy Spirit in the lives of those who walk closely with God. It is a fruit of the Spirit (Galatians 5:22), and it reflects a heart that has found its greatest treasure in the Lord.

Teaching (Part 2):

Joy is a spiritual posture of contentment and trust. James 1:2 challenges us to *"Consider it pure joy, my brothers and sisters, whenever you face trials of many kinds."* This joy is not denial of hardship, but confidence that God is using every trial to perfect and mature us.

Joy grows as we worship, pray, and meditate on God's Word. It is nurtured when we set our minds on eternal truths rather than temporary troubles. Paul, even in prison, could declare, *"Rejoice in the Lord always. I will say it again: Rejoice!"* (Philippians 4:4). His joy was not circumstantial; it was anchored in Christ.

A godly life is not free of trials but is filled with joy that transcends them. Joy in the Lord becomes our strength, our witness, and our reward. When we live in joy, we demonstrate to the world that God's presence is more satisfying than anything else life can offer.

Reflection Questions:

1. How would you define the difference between joy and happiness according to Scripture?

2. In what areas of your life do you need to invite God's joy?

3. How can you cultivate joy daily through worship, prayer, and Scripture?

4. Why is joy a powerful testimony to a watching world?

5. Write a prayer asking God to fill you with His joy, regardless of your circumstances.

Closing Prayer:

"Father, thank You for the joy that can only be found in Your presence. Teach me to draw strength from You daily, to rejoice in every circumstance, and to trust that You are working all things for my good. Let my life radiate the unshakable joy that comes from knowing You. In Jesus' name, Amen."

Verses for Meditation:

- **Nehemiah 8:10** — *"The joy of the Lord is your strength."*
- **Psalm 16:11** — *"You make known to me the path of life; in your presence there is fullness of joy."*
- **Galatians 5:22** — *"But the fruit of the Spirit is love, joy, peace, forbearance, kindness, goodness, faithfulness."*
- **James 1:2** — *"Consider it pure joy, my brothers and sisters, whenever you face trials of many kinds."*
- **Philippians 4:4** — *"Rejoice in the Lord always. I will say it again: Rejoice!"*

Key Takeaways:

- Joy is found in God's presence and is not dependent on circumstances.
- True joy is a fruit of the Spirit and a powerful source of strength.
- Joy reflects a heart that trusts God fully and rejoices in His unchanging character.

Real-Life Testimony:

After losing her husband unexpectedly, Mariah faced overwhelming grief. Yet, as she leaned into God's presence through worship and prayer, she experienced a peace and joy that surpassed understanding. Despite her pain, she smiled again, served others, and testified of God's sustaining joy. Her life is a beautiful reminder that true joy is not the absence of sorrow but the presence of God.

Chapter 18: Forgiveness – Letting Go for Freedom

Scripture:
"The discretion of a man makes him slow to anger, and his glory is to overlook a transgression." – Proverbs 19:11

Introduction:
Forgiveness is not condoning wrongdoing—it's releasing yourself from bitterness. It's choosing freedom over bondage and letting God heal what you can't fix. It reflects the mercy we've received from Christ.

Biblical Example:
Joseph forgave the brothers who betrayed him and provided for them during famine. His grace restored his family and demonstrated God's redemptive power. (Genesis 50:20–21)

Reflection Questions:
- Who do I need to forgive?
- What pain am I still holding onto?
- How has God forgiven me?

Practical Wisdom for Today:
- Forgiveness is a choice, not a feeling.
- Let go and trust God with the justice.
- Keep forgiving, even if it's daily.

Real-Life Story:
I struggled for years to forgive someone who hurt me deeply. But through prayer and surrender, God softened my heart. Forgiveness didn't erase the pain, but it set me free.

Biblical Person Who Did:
Joseph – extended forgiveness and provision.

Biblical Person Who Didn't:
King Saul – refused to release bitterness toward David and became tormented.

Key Verses to Reflect On:
- Matthew 6:14–15
- Colossians 3:13
- Ephesians 4:31–32

Prayer:
Lord, help me to forgive as You have forgiven me. Heal the wounds I can't see and free me from resentment. In Jesus name, Amen.

Call to Action:
Write a letter of forgiveness—even if you never send it—and release the offense to God.

Teaching (Part 1):

Forgiveness is a command, not a suggestion, and it is key to living in freedom. Ephesians 4:32 urges us, *"Be kind and compassionate to one another, forgiving each other, just as in Christ God forgave you."* Forgiveness releases us from the chains of bitterness and frees us to walk in the fullness of God's grace.

Forgiveness does not excuse wrongdoing, nor does it always lead to restored relationships. It is a choice to release the offense to God and trust Him to heal and bring justice. When we forgive, we reflect the heart of God, who has forgiven us more than we could ever repay.

Teaching (Part 2)

Unforgiveness poisons the soul. It festers, breeding anger, resentment, and division. Jesus taught that we must forgive not seven times, but seventy times seven (Matthew 18:22) — a call to limitless grace.

Forgiveness is not a feeling; it is an act of obedience. As we forgive, God heals our wounds and renews our hearts. Living a godly life requires letting go of past hurts so that we can move forward in freedom and peace. Forgiveness is the door through which healing walks.

Reflection Questions:

1. What does forgiveness mean to you according to God's Word?

2. Why is forgiveness essential for spiritual freedom?

3. Are there offenses you are still holding onto that you need to release to God?

4. How has unforgiveness impacted your peace or relationships?

5. Write a prayer asking God for the strength and grace to forgive.

Closing Prayer:

"Lord, thank You for the forgiveness You have freely given me. Help me to forgive others as You have forgiven me. Heal my wounds, soften my heart, and set me free from bitterness. Let forgiveness flow from my life as a testimony of Your grace. In Jesus' name, Amen."

Verses for Meditation:

- **Ephesians 4:32** — *"Be kind and compassionate to one another, forgiving each other, just as in Christ God forgave you."*
- **Matthew 6:14** — *"For if you forgive other people when they sin against you, your heavenly Father will also forgive you."*
- **Colossians 3:13** — *"Forgive as the Lord forgave you."*

Key Takeaways:

- Forgiveness is a decision to release offenses and walk in freedom.
- It reflects God's grace and opens the door for healing.
- Forgiveness is essential for spiritual growth and peace.

Real-Life Testimony:

After years of carrying resentment toward a former friend, Isaac finally chose to forgive. It wasn't easy, but as he released the hurt to God, he experienced an unexpected peace and healing in his heart. His relationships improved, and his faith deepened. Isaac learned firsthand that forgiveness is not a gift to others — it's a gift to yourself.

Chapter 19: Gratitude – Living a Thankful Life

Scripture:
"A man's pride will bring him low, but the humble in spirit will retain honor." – Proverbs 29:23

Introduction:
Gratitude shifts our perspective and draws us closer to God. It helps us see His hand in the ordinary and strengthens our faith in difficult seasons.

Biblical Example:
The one leper out of ten returned to thank Jesus after being healed. His gratitude marked him, and Jesus honored his faith. (Luke 17:11–19)

Reflection Questions:
- Do I take time to thank God daily?
- What blessings have I overlooked?
- How does gratitude impact my faith?

Practical Wisdom for Today:
- Keep a daily gratitude list.
- Say "thank You" to God out loud.
- Share your testimony—it multiplies thanksgiving.

Real-Life Story:
In a time of financial strain, I began thanking God for every meal, every paid bill. My focus shifted from lack to provision, and peace followed.

Biblical Person Who Did:
The healed leper – returned with th

Biblical Person Who Didn't:

The other nine lepers – received healing but didn't express gratitude.

Key Verses to Reflect On:

- 1 Thessalonians 5:18
- Psalm 107:1
- Colossians 3:15

Prayer:

Father, thank You for Your constant blessings. Forgive me for complaining. Teach me to be thankful in every circumstance. In Jesus name, Amen.

Call to Action:

Each night this week, write down three things you're grateful for and thank God for them.

Teaching (Part 1):

Gratitude is the attitude that transforms ordinary living into extraordinary praise. 1 Thessalonians 5:18 commands, *"Give thanks in all circumstances; for this is God's will for you in Christ Jesus."* Gratitude shifts our focus from what we lack to what we have, from complaints to contentment, from worry to worship.

A thankful heart acknowledges God's hand in every season — in blessing and in trial. Gratitude is not dependent on perfect circumstances but on the unchanging goodness of God. It is a continual act of faith, trusting that God is working all things for our good, even when we cannot see it.

Teaching (Part 2)

Gratitude is a powerful defense against negativity and despair. It aligns our hearts with God's promises and cultivates joy, peace, and resilience. Psalm 107:1 says, *"Give thanks to the Lord, for he is good; his love endures forever."*

Practicing gratitude daily rewires our perspective and invites God's presence into every part of our lives. A godly life is marked by an ongoing rhythm of thanksgiving — a heart that chooses to bless the Lord at all times (Psalm 34:1).

Reflection Questions:

1. How do you define gratitude according to God's Word?

2. What are the benefits of practicing daily gratitude?

3. In what difficult areas can you choose to be thankful today?

4. How does gratitude change your perspective and deepen your faith?

5. Write a prayer thanking God for His blessings, seen and unseen.

Closing Prayer:

"Father, thank You for every blessing — the seen and the unseen. Teach me to live with a heart of gratitude, rejoicing in Your goodness in every season. Help me to give thanks in all circumstances and to glorify You with a thankful spirit. In Jesus' name, Amen."

Verses for Meditation:

- **1 Thessalonians 5:18** — *"Give thanks in all circumstances; for this is God's will for you in Christ Jesus."*
- **Psalm 107:1** — *"Give thanks to the Lord, for he is good; his love endures forever."*
- **Colossians 3:17** — *"And whatever you do, whether in word or deed, do it all in the name of the Lord Jesus, giving thanks to God the Father through him."*

Key Takeaways:

- Gratitude transforms our perspective and aligns us with God's heart.
- Thankfulness is an act of faith and trust in God's goodness.
- A life of gratitude invites joy, peace, and God's presence.

Real-Life Testimony:

Jenna began keeping a gratitude journal during a season of grief. Each day she listed three things she was thankful for, even when it was hard. Over time, her heart began to heal, and her outlook shifted from sorrow to hope. Gratitude didn't change her circumstances immediately, but it changed her — and that made all the difference.

Chapter 20: Compassion – Love That Acts

Scripture:
"He who has pity on the poor lends to the Lord, and He will pay back what he has given." – Proverbs 19:17

Introduction:
Compassion sees, feels, and acts. It's love in motion—responding to others' pain with presence, care, and action. God's compassion is what saved us—and we're called to extend it to others.

Biblical Example:
Jesus had compassion on the crowds and healed their sick, fed the hungry, and taught the lost. His compassion was constant and active. (Matthew 9:36, 14:14)

Reflection Questions:
- Where am I overlooking someone's need?
- Do I take time to truly see and care for people?
- How can I be more available to help others?

Practical Wisdom for Today:
- Compassion doesn't always need words—presence matters.
- Take time to notice and respond.
- Give generously—your time, resources, and empathy.

Real-Life Story:
I met a woman who had recently lost her home. Though I couldn't solve everything, I listened, encouraged, and helped connect her to resources. That simple compassion reminded her she wasn't alone.

Biblical Person Who Did:
Jesus – always moved with compassion.

Biblical Person Who Didn't:

The rich man – ignored Lazarus at his gate, and suffered the consequences. (Luke 16:19–31)

Key Verses to Reflect On:
- Zechariah 7:9
- Colossians 3:12
- 1 John 3:17–18

Prayer:

Lord, break my heart for what breaks Yours. Help me to love not just in words but in action. Make me sensitive to the needs around me. In Jesus name, Amen.

Call to Action:

Find someone in need this week and offer practical help—big or small—with love.

Teaching (Part 1):

Compassion is love in action. It is more than feeling sympathy — it is being moved to respond. Colossians 3:12 urges us, *"Clothe yourselves with compassion, kindness, humility, gentleness, and patience."*

Compassion sees the need and does something about it. It reflects the heart of God, who sent His Son because He *"so loved the world."* Jesus was often "moved with compassion" before healing, feeding, or comforting. Compassion is the bridge between feeling and doing — the fuel that drives the hands and feet of Christ.

Teaching (Part 2)

God calls us not only to care but to act — to feed the hungry, visit the sick, care for the hurting, and love the marginalized. Compassion is not convenient; it's costly. It requires time, energy, and sometimes sacrifice.

Yet when we love with action, we display the Gospel most clearly. 1 John 3:18 reminds us, *"Let us not love with words or speech but with actions and in truth."* A godly life is marked by compassion that moves beyond good intentions into powerful, tangible expressions of God's love.

Reflection Questions:

1. How do you define compassion according to God's Word?

2. What does it mean to love with action and truth?

3. Who in your life needs to experience God's compassion through you?

4. How can compassion deepen your walk with Christ and your witness to others?

5. Write a prayer asking God to help you respond to needs with His love in action.

Closing Prayer:

"Lord, fill my heart with Your compassion. Teach me to see others as You see them and to love not just with words, but with actions. Help me to be Your hands and feet, reaching those who are hurting with Your grace and mercy. In Jesus' name, Amen."

Verses for Meditation:

- **Colossians 3:12** — *"Clothe yourselves with compassion, kindness, humility, gentleness, and patience."*
- **1 John 3:18** — *"Let us not love with words or speech but with actions and in truth."*
- **Matthew 9:36** — *"When He saw the crowds, He had compassion on them, because they were harassed and helpless, like sheep without a shepherd."*

Key Takeaways:

- Compassion moves beyond feelings into action.
- True compassion reflects God's love and the Gospel.
- Love in action has the power to change lives and reveal Christ to the world.

Real-Life Testimony:

When Katrina volunteered at a shelter, she initially thought she was simply helping others. But over time, she realized compassion was changing her too — softening her heart and deepening her faith. Her small acts of kindness led many to ask about her hope, giving her a platform to share the love of Christ. Compassion became her ministry.

Chapter 21: Faithfulness – Steadfast in Spirit

Scripture:
 "A faithful man will abound with blessings, but he who hastens to be rich will not go unpunished." – Proverbs 28:20

Introduction:
Faithfulness is the steady commitment to God's ways, regardless of circumstances. It's being trustworthy, dependable, and consistent—even when no one is watching. God honors faithfulness.

Biblical Example:
Ruth stayed with Naomi and worked hard in the fields. Her faithfulness led to redemption and positioned her in the lineage of Christ. (Ruth 1–4)

Reflection Questions:
- Am I consistent in my walk with God?
- Do I keep my word even when it's inconvenient?
- What small task has God called me to be faithful in?

Practical Wisdom for Today:
- Do what is right even when no one sees.
- Be faithful in the small things.
- Trust that God rewards obedience over time.

Real-Life Story:
I served for years in a behind-the-scenes role. It didn't feel impactful at first, but people began to comment on the difference my consistency made. God used it more than I realized.

Biblical Person Who Did:
Ruth – remained loyal and steady.

Biblical Person Who Didn't:

Judas Iscariot – betrayed Jesus for money, abandoning his calling.

Key Verses to Reflect On:

- Luke 16:10
- Galatians 6:9
- 1 Corinthians 4:2

Prayer:

Lord, help me to remain faithful in all I do. Let my heart be anchored in Your truth, and let my life reflect Your steadfast love. In Jesus name, Amen.

Call to Action:

Choose one small area—devotions, work, family—and commit to faithfulness this week without recognition.

Teaching (Part 1):

Faithfulness is a rare treasure — a steady, unwavering commitment that endures through every season. Proverbs 3:3–4 instructs us, *"Let love and faithfulness never leave you; bind them around your neck, write them on the tablet of your heart. Then you will win favor and a good name in the sight of God and man."*

Faithfulness is not tested in comfort; it is proven in adversity. To be faithful is to remain constant in devotion — to God, to our calling, and to the people He entrusts to us — even when it costs us something. In a culture of convenience, God calls His children to a higher standard: steadfastness that mirrors His own unchanging character.

A faithful spirit is not fickle, shifting with emotions or circumstances. It is anchored in the truth of God's Word and fueled by love for Him. Those who are faithful in the little will be entrusted with much (Luke 16:10).

Teaching (Part 2):

God's faithfulness is our model and our motivation. Lamentations 3:22–23 reminds us, *"Because of the Lord's great love we are not consumed, for his compassions never fail. They are new every morning; great is your faithfulness."*

Just as God remains faithful to His promises, we are called to be faithful in ours — in marriage, friendships, ministry, work, and worship. Faithfulness shows up in small, daily choices: keeping our word, showing up, staying true to our commitments, and serving when it's hard or unnoticed.

Faithfulness is not flashy, but it is powerful. It builds trust, strengthens relationships, and cultivates character. A godly life is marked by enduring loyalty to God's purposes — holding fast to Him and His call even when feelings waver or the results aren't immediate. Faithfulness is the soil where fruitfulness grows.

Reflection Questions:

1. How does God's faithfulness inspire you to be faithful in your own life?

2. In what areas is God calling you to remain steadfast, even when it's difficult?

3. What small daily habits can help cultivate faithfulness in your walk with God?

4. Why is faithfulness important in both personal and spiritual growth?

5. Write a prayer asking God to strengthen your heart to remain faithful in all seasons.

Closing Prayer:

"Lord, thank You for Your unchanging faithfulness. Teach me to reflect Your steadfast love in my life. Strengthen my heart to stay faithful to You and to the assignments You have given me. Help me to stand firm in every season, knowing that You are faithful to complete what You have begun. In Jesus' name, Amen."

Verses for Meditation:

- **Proverbs 3:3–4** — *"Let love and faithfulness never leave you; bind them around your neck, write them on the tablet of your heart."*
- **Lamentations 3:22–23** — *"Great is your faithfulness."*
- **Luke 16:10** — *"Whoever can be trusted with very little can also be trusted with much."*
- **1 Corinthians 4:2** — *"Now it is required that those who have been given a trust must prove faithful."*
- **2 Thessalonians 3:3** — *"But the Lord is faithful, and he will strengthen you and protect you from the evil one."*

Key Takeaways:

- Faithfulness is steadfastness in devotion to God and His purposes.
- God's unchanging faithfulness is the model and motivation for our own.
- Daily decisions of obedience and loyalty cultivate lasting fruitfulness.

Real-Life Testimony:

Carlos served quietly in his church for over twenty years — setting up chairs, cleaning floors, mentoring young believers. He was never in the spotlight, but his faithfulness built a legacy. Generations of believers were strengthened by his steady presence and encouragement. Today, his story reminds us that lasting impact comes not from grand gestures but from simple, daily faithfulness over time — a reflection of God's enduring love.

Chapter 22: Boldness – Courage Rooted in Conviction

Scripture:
"The wicked flee when no one pursues, but the righteous are bold as a lion." – Proverbs 28:1

Introduction:
Boldness in Christ is not arrogance—it's Spirit-empowered courage to stand for truth and live unashamedly for God.

Biblical Example:
Peter and John boldly preached Jesus even when threatened by religious leaders. They declared, "We cannot help speaking about what we have seen and heard." (Acts 4:13–20)

Reflection Questions:
- Am I bold in sharing my faith?
- Where do I feel fear is holding me back?
- How can I grow in spiritual confidence?

Practical Wisdom for Today:
- Speak truth in love.
- Spend time in prayer before stepping into bold moments.
- Remember who you represent—Jesus.

Real-Life Story:
I once hesitated to pray for a coworker publicly. But when I finally did, it opened a door for deeper conversation and faith-sharing.

Biblical Person Who Did:
Peter – preached boldly after the resurrection.

Biblical Person Who Didn't:

Pontius Pilate – feared people more than truth and handed over Jesus.

Key Verses to Reflect On:
- 2 Timothy 1:7
- Ephesians 6:19–20
- Acts 4:29

Prayer:

Father, give me boldness to speak and live for You. Fill me with courage to follow Your lead even when it costs me. In Jesus name, Amen.

Call to Action:

Take one bold step this week—share your faith, pray aloud, or speak truth in love.

Teaching (Part 1):

Boldness is not recklessness — it is courage anchored in godly conviction. Proverbs 28:1 declares, *"The wicked flee though no one pursues, but the righteous are as bold as a lion."* Boldness comes from knowing who we are in Christ and what we stand for according to His truth.

Biblical boldness is the willingness to speak truth, live righteously, and act in obedience to God, even in the face of fear, opposition, or uncertainty. It is not arrogance or stubbornness; it is a quiet strength fueled by deep trust in God's promises.

Throughout Scripture, boldness was the hallmark of those who changed history — Moses standing before Pharaoh, David facing Goliath, Esther risking her life before the king, and the apostles proclaiming the Gospel in defiance of persecution. Their boldness was not based on self-confidence, but on confidence in God.

Teaching (Part 2):

True boldness grows out of intimacy with God. Acts 4:13 records that the religious leaders were astonished at the boldness of Peter and John, recognizing that they had *been with Jesus.* Boldness is not something we muster up on our own; it is the overflow of knowing God's character and being filled with His Spirit.

Boldness rooted in conviction enables us to stand firm in a world of compromise. It empowers us to proclaim truth in love and to pursue God's calling without wavering. 2 Timothy 1:7 reminds us, *"For God gave us a spirit not of fear but of power and love and self-control."*

A godly life is marked by a boldness that glorifies God — a boldness to love fearlessly, to serve sacrificially, and to proclaim the Gospel unashamedly. Boldness, when grounded in conviction and guided by love, becomes a powerful witness to the world around us.

Reflection Questions:

1. How would you define boldness according to Scripture?

2. In what areas is God calling you to step out in boldness?

3. How can spending time with God strengthen your boldness?

4. What fears often hold you back from bold obedience?

5. Write a prayer asking God to fill you with boldness rooted in conviction and love.

Closing Prayer:

"Lord, fill me with boldness that comes from knowing You deeply. Teach me to stand firm in Your truth, to speak with courage, and to act in obedience even when it is hard. Let my life be marked by bold conviction and gentle love, reflecting Your heart to the world. In Jesus' name, Amen."

Verses for Meditation:

- **Proverbs 28:1** — *"The wicked flee though no one pursues, but the righteous are as bold as a lion."*
- **Acts 4:13** — *"When they saw the boldness of Peter and John... they were astonished and they recognized that they had been with Jesus."*
- **2 Timothy 1:7** — *"For God gave us a spirit not of fear but of power and love and self-control."*
- **Ephesians 6:19–20** — *"Pray also for me, that whenever I speak, words may be given me so that I will fearlessly make known the mystery of the gospel."*
- **Joshua 1:9** — *"Be strong and courageous. Do not be afraid; do not be discouraged, for the Lord your God will be with you wherever you go."*

Key Takeaways:

- Boldness is courage rooted not in self, but in God's truth and presence.
- True boldness comes from time spent with Jesus and being filled with the Holy Spirit.
- Godly boldness empowers us to proclaim truth and live righteously without fear.

Real-Life Testimony:

Amira struggled with fear of sharing her faith at work. She began to pray for boldness, asking God for opportunities to speak. Over time, God opened doors for conversations, and Amira learned to trust the Spirit's prompting. Her gentle, bold witness led two coworkers to Christ. Amira's story shows that boldness rooted in conviction can open eternal doors and glorify God in powerful ways.

Chapter 23: Honesty – Living Without Deceit

Scripture:
"Lying lips are an abomination to the Lord, but those who deal truthfully are His delight." – Proverbs 12:22

Introduction:
Honesty reflects the integrity and light of Christ. In a world of half-truths and hidden motives, honesty builds trust and honors God.

Biblical Example:
Jesus always spoke the truth—even when it offended others. He declared, "I am the way, the truth, and the life." (John 14:6)

Reflection Questions:
- Am I honest in small things as well as big?
- Do I speak truth with grace?
- What area of my life needs more transparency?

Practical Wisdom for Today:
- Tell the truth, even when it's difficult.
- Avoid exaggeration or withholding information.
- Let your life be consistent with your words.

Real-Life Story:
There was a situation where I could have stayed silent about a mistake. But I chose to confess. Though it was hard, it brought healing and deeper respect.

Biblical Person Who Did:
Jesus – embodied truth in every word.

Biblical Person Who Didn't:
Ananias and Sapphira – lied about their giving and paid with their lives.

Key Verses to Reflect On:
- Proverbs 10:9
- Ephesians 4:25
- Colossians 3:9

Prayer:
Lord, make me a person of truth. Remove every trace of deceit from my heart. Let my words and life reflect Your integrity. In Jesus name, Amen.

Call to Action:
Examine your speech and actions this week. Confess any dishonesty and make it right.

Teaching (Part 1):

Honesty is the foundation of a life that honors God. Proverbs 12:22 says, *"The Lord detests lying lips, but he delights in people who are trustworthy."* God is a God of truth, and those who walk with Him are called to reflect His truthfulness in every word and action.

Living with honesty means being truthful in speech, transparent in actions, and genuine in character. It requires integrity even when no one is watching, and trustworthiness even when honesty may cost us something. Deceit destroys trust, fractures relationships, and distances us from God's blessings.

An honest life invites peace — there is no fear of exposure or shame. It builds credibility and opens doors for God's favor. Those who walk in truth walk in freedom, because dishonesty always leads to bondage. Honesty reflects the very heart of God and leads us into deeper intimacy with Him.

Teaching (Part 2):

Jesus Himself declared, *"I am the way and the truth and the life"* (John 14:6). As followers of Christ, we are called not only to speak truth but to live truthfully. Honesty is not just about avoiding lies — it's about living with authenticity and integrity in every area of life.

Ephesians 4:25 commands us to *"put off falsehood and speak truthfully to your neighbor, for we are all members of one body."* When we live honestly, we honor the image of God in ourselves and in others. Honesty strengthens the community, builds lasting relationships, and protects our witness to a watching world.

Deceit may seem like a shortcut to avoid consequences or gain advantage, but it ultimately leads to destruction. A godly life is marked by a deep commitment to truth — not situational truth, but God's truth, unchanging and eternal. In a world filled with compromise and half-truths, honesty shines brightly for Christ.

Reflection Questions:

1. How does living honestly reflect the character of God?

2. In what areas is God challenging you to walk in greater honesty?

3. How does deceit damage relationships and hinder spiritual growth?

4. What are some practical ways to cultivate honesty in your daily life?

5. Write a prayer asking God to give you a heart committed to truth in all things.

Closing Prayer:

"Father, You are the God of truth. Help me to walk in honesty and integrity, reflecting Your character in all that I do. Give me the courage to speak the truth in love and to live with authenticity. Guard my heart against deceit, and let my life be a light that points others to You. In Jesus' name, Amen."

Verses for Meditation:

- **Proverbs 12:22** — *"The Lord detests lying lips, but he delights in people who are trustworthy."*
- **John 14:6** — *"I am the way and the truth and the life."*
- **Ephesians 4:25** — *"Therefore each of you must put off falsehood and speak truthfully to your neighbor."*
- **Psalm 15:2** — *"The one whose walk is blameless, who does what is righteous, who speaks the truth from their heart."*
- **Colossians 3:9–10** — *"Do not lie to each other, since you have taken off your old self with its practices and have put on the new self."*

Key Takeaways:

- Honesty is the foundation of a life that honors and reflects God.
- Truthfulness builds trust, strengthens relationships, and protects our witnesses.
- Deceit leads to destruction; honesty leads to freedom, peace, and God's favor.

Real-Life Testimony:

Ben once struggled with cutting corners and hiding mistakes at work to protect his reputation. After coming under conviction, he chose to walk in honesty, even when it meant admitting errors. Over time, his honesty earned him the respect of his colleagues and led to unexpected promotions. Ben's story shows that honesty, though costly in the short term, brings lasting blessing and favor from God.

Chapter 24: Reverence – Honoring God in All Things

Scripture:
"The fear of the Lord is a fountain of life, to turn one away from the snares of death." – Proverbs 14:27

Introduction:
Reverence is deep respect for God's holiness. It causes us to worship, obey, and live with awareness of His majesty. Reverence keeps us aligned with His will.

Biblical Example:
Isaiah saw a vision of God's glory and cried, "Woe is me!" His reverence changed his calling. (Isaiah 6:1–8)

Reflection Questions:
- Do I approach God casually or with awe?
- How do I express reverence in my worship and conduct?
- What habits reflect a fear of the Lord in my life?

Practical Wisdom for Today:
- Worship daily and sincerely.
- Speak of God with honor.
- Live in obedience—not just belief.

Real-Life Story:
Reverence became real to me when I stood at a hospital bedside, praying. I sensed God's presence so strongly that all I could do was bow and cry. That moment blessed my soul.

Biblical Person Who Did:
Isaiah – responded to God with holy fear.

Biblical Person Who Didn't:
Nadab and Abihu – offered unauthorized fire and were consumed for dishonoring God.

Key Verses to Reflect On:
- Hebrews 12:28
- Psalm 111:10
- Ecclesiastes 12:13

Prayer:
Holy God, teach me to live with reverence. Let my heart stand in awe of who You are. May I never take Your grace lightly. In Jesus name, Amen.

Call to Action:
Take time this week to reflect on God's majesty. Worship Him with reverence in a quiet place.

Teaching (Part 1):

Reverence is the deep respect, awe, and honor we show to God because of who He is. Hebrews 12:28 urges us, *"Therefore, since we are receiving a kingdom that cannot be shaken, let us be thankful, and so worship God acceptably with reverence and awe."* Reverence shapes the way we approach God, worship Him, and live before Him daily.

Reverence is not fear that drives us away but awe that draws us nearer. It is recognizing His majesty, His holiness, and His authority over our lives. True reverence leads to worship — not just in songs or prayers but in a lifestyle that honors God in every decision, action, and thought.

When we revere God, we take His Word seriously, we honor His name in our speech, and we submit to His will even when it is difficult. Reverence leads to obedience because we recognize God's wisdom is higher than ours. A heart filled with reverence gives God His rightful place — above everything else.

Teaching (Part 2):

Reverence affects every area of our lives — from how we worship to how we treat others, to how we carry out our daily responsibilities. Proverbs 9:10 reminds us, *"The fear of the Lord is the beginning of wisdom, and knowledge of the Holy One is understanding."*

In a culture that often takes God lightly, reverence sets us apart. It reminds us that God is not casual — He is holy, sovereign, and worthy of our utmost respect. Reverence acknowledges that every blessing we have is from Him and that our lives are to be lived for His glory, not our own.

A life of reverence is a life that says, *"Lord, not my will, but Yours be done."* It transforms our worship into more than songs — it becomes a daily offering. Reverence cultivates humility, deepens our intimacy with God, and positions us to receive His guidance and blessing.

Reflection Questions:

1. What does it mean to live with reverence toward God in your daily life?

2. How does reverence impact your worship, decisions, and relationships?

3. In what areas is God inviting you to show greater honor and respect for Him?

4. Why is reverence the beginning of true wisdom?

5. Write a prayer asking God to cultivate a deeper reverence for Him in your heart and life.

Closing Prayer:

"Father, You are holy, sovereign, and worthy of all honor. Teach me to live with deep reverence for You. Let my life be a reflection of Your greatness and goodness. Fill my heart with awe and my life with obedience, that I may honor You in all that I do. In Jesus' name, Amen."

Verses for Meditation:

- **Hebrews 12:28** — *"Worship God acceptably with reverence and awe."*
- **Proverbs 9:10** — *"The fear of the Lord is the beginning of wisdom."*
- **Ecclesiastes 12:13** — *"Fear God and keep his commandments, for this is the duty of all mankind."*
- **Psalm 89:7** — *"In the council of the holy ones God is greatly feared; he is more awesome than all who surround him."*
- **Malachi 1:6** — *"If I am a father, where is the honor due me? If I am a master, where is the respect due me?" says the Lord Almighty.*

Key Takeaways:

- Reverence is honoring God's holiness, authority, and greatness in every area of life.
- True reverence leads to obedience, humility, and deeper intimacy with God.
- A reverent life shines in a world that has forgotten the awe of God.

Real-Life Testimony:

Samantha grew up attending church but often treated her faith casually. As she matured, she began to study the attributes of God — His holiness, sovereignty, and majesty. This understanding led to a shift in her heart. Worship became more meaningful, obedience more urgent, and her entire life transformed into an act of reverence. Now, she mentors young women, teaching them to live lives that honor God in all things — proving that reverence reshapes not just our relationship with God but every aspect of how we live.

Chapter 25: Perseverance – Enduring in Faith

Scripture:
"The righteous falls seven times and rises again..." – Proverbs 24:16

Introduction:
Perseverance is the ability to keep going when it's hard. It's choosing to believe, serve, and obey even when there's no applause. It's faithfulness over time that produces godly fruit.

Biblical Example:
Job lost everything but did not curse God. He endured grief, suffering, and silence but held onto faith. In the end, God restored him. (Job 1–42)

Reflection Questions:
- What have I given up on too soon?
- Do I press through hardship or retreat?
- How does God strengthen me to persevere?

Practical Wisdom for Today:
- Keep praying, even in silence.
- Don't judge your walk by your feelings.
- Trust God's promise more than your pain.

Real-Life Story:
I once wanted to quit an assignment. It felt unfruitful. But through prayer, I stayed. Months later, the breakthrough came—and I realized the blessing was tied to staying.

Biblical Person Who Did:
Job – held on to faith through extreme trials.

Biblical Person Who Didn't:

Demas – abandoned Paul because he loved the world.

Key Verses to Reflect On:

- James 1:12
- Romans 5:3–5
- Galatians 6:9

Prayer:

Lord, give me strength to endure. Help me to remain faithful, even when the way is long. Let my perseverance bring glory to You. In Jesus name, Amen.

Call to Action:

Write down what you're tempted to give up on. Ask God for grace to keep going—and take one step forward this week.

Teaching (Part 1):

Perseverance is the steady, unwavering commitment to continue in faith, regardless of opposition or hardship. James 1:12 promises, *"Blessed is the one who perseveres under trial because, having stood the test, that person will receive the crown of life that the Lord has promised to those who love him."*

Perseverance is not passive endurance; it is active, courageous faithfulness to God's calling. It means holding tightly to God's promises when circumstances scream otherwise. Trials are not obstacles to faith — they are the proving grounds where perseverance is forged.

Faith that endures is faith that matures. God uses seasons of hardship to refine us, deepen our trust in Him, and grow our spiritual character. Without perseverance, faith remains shallow; with it, faith becomes unshakable. Perseverance transforms temporary suffering into eternal glory.

Teaching (Part 2):

Hebrews 12:1–2 encourages us to *"run with perseverance the race marked out for us, fixing our eyes on Jesus, the pioneer and perfecter of faith."* Perseverance requires focus — not on our struggles, but on our Savior.

Enduring in faith means trusting that God's promises are true even when they seem distant. It means continuing to pray, worship, and obey when feelings waver. It is fueled not by human strength, but by divine grace — the strength that God supplies daily.

A godly life is not defined by how well we start but by how faithfully we finish. Perseverance is a testimony to the world that Christ is worth every hardship. It is an act of worship — a declaration that our faith rests not on what is seen, but on the unchanging faithfulness of God.

Reflection Questions:

1. What does perseverance in faith look like in your current season of life?

2. How can you fix your eyes on Jesus when you feel like giving up?

3. What lessons has God taught you through trials that required perseverance?

4. How can the hope of eternal rewards encourage you to endure today's hardships?

5. Write a prayer asking God to strengthen your perseverance and faith.

Closing Prayer:

"Father, give me the strength to endure in faith no matter what trials I face. Teach me to fix my eyes on Jesus and to trust in Your promises even when the road is long and hard. Let perseverance produce maturity in me, and let my life glorify You as I walk faithfully to the finish. In Jesus' name, Amen."

Verses for Meditation:

- **James 1:12** — *"Blessed is the one who perseveres under trial."*
- **Hebrews 12:1–2** — *"Let us run with perseverance the race marked out for us, fixing our eyes on Jesus."*
- **Romans 5:3–4** — *"Suffering produces perseverance; perseverance, character; and character, hope."*
- **Galatians 6:9** — *"Let us not become weary in doing good, for at the proper time we will reap a harvest if we do not give up."*
- **2 Timothy 4:7** — *"I have fought the good fight, I have finished the race, I have kept the faith."*

Key Takeaways:

- Perseverance is enduring faith that grows stronger through trials.
- God uses hardship to refine us and prepare us for eternal rewards.
- Enduring in faith glorifies God and strengthens our testimony to others.

Real-Life Testimony:

Leah faced a long battle with chronic illness that left her exhausted and discouraged. Yet through it all, she chose to cling to God's promises, even when answers didn't come quickly. Over the years, Leah's unwavering perseverance inspired her church and family. She often said, "Even if healing doesn't come in this life, I have already won in Christ." Leah's story is a powerful reminder that enduring in faith, even through pain, brings glory to God and hope to others.

Chapter 26: Discernment – Seeing with Spiritual Clarity

Scripture:
"The simple believes every word, but the prudent considers well his steps." – Proverbs 14:15

Introduction:
Discernment is the ability to judge rightly between truth and error, good and best. It's a gift from God that helps us avoid deception and walk wisely.

Biblical Example:
Solomon used discernment to identify the true mother of a child by proposing to divide the baby. The real mother's response revealed the truth. (1 Kings 3:16–28)

Reflection Questions:
- Do I seek God's insight before making decisions?
- How do I test the voices and influences in my life?
- Am I growing in spiritual sensitivity?

Practical Wisdom for Today:
- Ask the Holy Spirit for discernment.
- Weigh decisions against Scripture.
- Don't ignore godly counsel.

Real-Life Story:
I once considered a partnership that looked great on the surface. Through prayer and wise counsel, I saw red flags and declined. Months later, the truth came out. Discernment protected me.

Biblical Person Who Did:
Solomon – applied discernment in leadership.

Biblical Person Who Didn't:
The Galatians – were swayed by false teaching (Galatians 3:1).

Key Verses to Reflect On:
- Hebrews 5:14
- 1 Thessalonians 5:21–22
- James 1:5

Prayer:
Lord, give me a discerning heart. Help me recognize Your voice and resist confusion. May I walk wisely and honor You in every choice. In Jesus name, Amen.

Call to Action:
Before making any key decision this week, stop and pray for discernment—then wait for God's direction.

Teaching (Part 1):

Discernment is the spiritual ability to distinguish between truth and error, right and wrong, God's voice and deception. Hebrews 5:14 tells us, *"But solid food is for the mature, who by constant use have trained themselves to distinguish good from evil."* Discernment is not merely intellectual — it is spiritual sensitivity sharpened by God's Word and the Holy Spirit.

In a world flooded with conflicting voices, discernment is essential for navigating life wisely. It guards us against deception, keeps us aligned with God's will, and protects our hearts from compromise. Without discernment, we are easily swayed by appearance, emotion, or human reasoning.

A discerning spirit sees beyond what is obvious. It listens for God's direction in every decision and recognizes the spiritual realities behind physical circumstances. Discernment is a gift but also a skill that grows as we mature in Christ.

Teaching (Part 2):

Discernment is closely linked to intimacy with God. John 10:27 says, *"My sheep listen to my voice; I know them, and they follow me."* The more time we spend in God's presence and Word, the clearer His voice becomes and the more attuned we are to His leading.

Discernment enables us to test what we hear, see, and experience against the truth of Scripture. 1 John 4:1 instructs, *"Dear friends, do not believe every spirit, but test the spirits to see whether they are from God."* Discernment also helps us choose relationships, opportunities, and paths that align with God's purposes.

A godly life is not driven by impulse but led by discernment. Spiritual clarity helps us avoid the traps of the enemy and walk confidently in God's will. Discernment is a light in the darkness, guiding us with wisdom and protecting us with truth.

Reflection Questions:

1. How would you describe spiritual discernment in your own words?

2. What practices can help you grow in discernment daily?

3. Why is discernment critical in today's culture?

4. In what areas of your life do you need clearer discernment right now?

5. Write a prayer asking God to sharpen your spiritual discernment and clarity.

Closing Prayer:

"Lord, open my eyes to see as You see. Sharpen my discernment so that I can distinguish truth from error and walk in Your wisdom. Teach me to listen carefully to Your voice and to test everything by Your Word. Protect my heart and mind from deception, and guide me in paths of righteousness. In Jesus' name, Amen."

Verses for Meditation:

- **Hebrews 5:14** — *"But solid food is for the mature, who by constant use have trained themselves to distinguish good from evil."*
- **John 10:27** — *"My sheep listen to my voice; I know them, and they follow me."*
- **1 John 4:1** — *"Dear friends, do not believe every spirit, but test the spirits to see whether they are from God."*
- **Philippians 1:9–10** — *"That your love may abound more and more in knowledge and depth of insight, so that you may be able to discern what is best."*
- **Proverbs 3:5–6** — *"Trust in the Lord with all your heart and lean not on your own understanding; in all your ways submit to him, and he will make your paths straight."*

Key Takeaways:

- Discernment is spiritual clarity that distinguishes truth from deception.
- It is developed through intimacy with God and constant use of His Word.
- A discerning life is a protected, guided life — aligned with God's purposes.

Real-Life Testimony:

Marcus was offered a high-paying job that seemed perfect on the surface. But as he prayed, he felt a check in his spirit. After seeking counsel and testing the opportunity against God's Word, he realized the role would compromise his values. Declining it wasn't easy, but months later, God opened a better door — one that honored his convictions and advanced his calling. Marcus's story is a reminder that discernment preserves destiny and honors God.

Chapter 27: Faith – Trusting Beyond What You See

Scripture:
"Trust in the Lord with all your heart, and lean not on your own understanding." – Proverbs 3:5

Introduction:
Faith is believing when we can't see and trusting when we don't understand. It's the foundation of a life that pleases God.

Biblical Example:
Abraham left his homeland not knowing where he was going. He trusted God's promise of a nation and waited for a son in old age. (Hebrews 11:8–12)

Reflection Questions:
- What situation is testing my faith right now?
- Am I leaning on God or my own logic?
- How can I deepen my trust in God's character?

Practical Wisdom for Today:
- Speak faith over your fears.
- Surround yourself with people of strong faith.
- Reflect on past answered prayers.

Real-Life Story:
I stepped out in faith to pursue a calling with no clear path. Though uncertain, I found peace and provision at every step. Faith didn't remove the risk, but it led to a reward.

Biblical Person Who Did:
Abraham – believed God's promise despite the odds.

Biblical Person Who Didn't:
The Israelites – feared entering the Promised Land and missed their blessing.

Key Verses to Reflect On:
- Hebrews 11:1
- Romans 4:20–21
- Mark 11:22–24

Prayer:
God, increase my faith. Help me to trust Your heart when I can't see Your hand. Let me walk boldly, believing You are who You say You are. In Jesus name, Amen.

Call to Action:
Take one step of faith this week—small or large—and write down what God does through it.

Teaching (Part 1):

Faith is the foundation of our relationship with God. Hebrews 11:1 defines it: *"Now faith is confidence in what we hope for and assurance about what we do not see."* Faith trusts in the unseen promises of God and rests in His unchanging character.

Living by faith means believing God's Word even when circumstances challenge it. It's trusting that God is who He says He is and will do what He has promised. Faith calls us to walk with confidence even when we don't see the full picture, knowing that our steps are ordered by the Lord (Psalm 37:23).

Faith is not a feeling; it is a firm conviction based on the reliability of God. It teaches us to lean not on our understanding but to rely wholly on Him. A life of faith is one that is anchored in trust — believing that God's plans are greater than our sight and His timing is always perfect.

Teaching (Part 2):

Faith is the currency of the Kingdom. Hebrews 11:6 reminds us, *"Without faith it is impossible to please God."* Faith moves mountains (Matthew 17:20), opens doors, and aligns us with the will of God. It demands obedience even when the outcome is unclear.

Faith grows through trials and testing. James 1:3 tells us, *"The testing of your faith produces perseverance."* Every challenge is an opportunity for faith to deepen, for trust to be strengthened, and for God's power to be revealed.

A godly life is not about seeing first and then believing — it's about believing first and trusting God with what is unseen. Faith anchors us in seasons of uncertainty and propels us forward when fear tries to hold us back. Trusting beyond what we see is not blind; it is grounded in the full assurance that God is faithful.

Reflection Questions:

1. How does Scripture define faith, and what does that mean in your life today?

2. In what areas is God calling you to trust Him beyond what you can see?

3. How can the trials you face help strengthen your faith?

4. Why is faith essential to pleasing God and walking in His promises?

5. Write a prayer asking God to deepen your faith and teach you to trust beyond sight.

Closing Prayer:

"Father, help me to trust You beyond what I can see. Teach me to walk by faith and not by sight, to lean on Your promises when my circumstances are uncertain. Strengthen my heart to believe in Your goodness and timing, even when the way is unclear. Let my life be a testimony of unwavering faith in Your unfailing love. In Jesus' name, Amen."

Verses for Meditation:

- **Hebrews 11:1** — *"Now faith is confidence in what we hope for and assurance about what we do not see."*
- **2 Corinthians 5:7** — *"For we live by faith, not by sight."*
- **Hebrews 11:6** — *"And without faith it is impossible to please God."*
- **Psalm 37:23** — *"The Lord makes firm the steps of the one who delights in him."*
- **Matthew 17:20** — *"If you have faith as small as a mustard seed... nothing will be impossible for you."*

Key Takeaways:

- Faith is trusting in God's promises even when they are unseen.
- Faith pleases God and is essential for walking in His will.
- Trials grow our faith and reveal the faithfulness of God.

Real-Life Testimony:

Daniel was offered an opportunity to start a ministry in a small, struggling community. He had no guaranteed support, no salary, and no certainty of success. But God had spoken, and Daniel chose to step out in faith. Over time, what started as a small act of trust blossomed into a thriving outreach that transformed lives. Daniel's story shows that trusting beyond what we see leads to blessings we could never imagine.

Chapter 28: Temperance – Living with Self-Control

Scripture:
"He who is slow to anger is better than the mighty, and he who rules his spirit than he who takes a city." – Proverbs 16:32

Introduction:
Temperance is the fruit of self-control. It keeps emotions, impulses, and desires in submission to God. It's not repression but Spirit-led discipline.

Biblical Example:
Daniel chose not to defile himself with the king's rich food. He exercised temperance and honored God above appetite. (Daniel 1:8–16)

Reflection Questions:
- What area of my life needs more self-control?
- Do I overreact or respond with grace?
- How can I develop spiritual discipline?

Practical Wisdom for Today:
- Pause before responding.
- Fast from distractions that weaken your focus.
- Let God shape your desires through prayer.

Real-Life Story:
I used to struggle with anger. Through prayer and accountability, I learned to pause and pray before responding. God has given me peace where rage once lived.

Biblical Person Who Did:
Daniel – restrained his appetite to honor God.

Biblical Person Who Didn't:
Esau – gave up his birthright to satisfy hunger.

Key Verses to Reflect On:
- Galatians 5:22–23
- 1 Corinthians 9:25–27
- Proverbs 25:28

Prayer:
Lord, help me master my spirit. Fill me with the fruit of self-control. Let my life reflect Your discipline and peace. In Jesus name, Amen.

Call to Action:
Identify one habit to surrender and one godly habit to build in its place this week.

Teaching (Part 1):

Temperance, or self-control, is the disciplined mastery of desires, emotions, and actions. Proverbs 25:28 warns, *"Like a city whose walls are broken through is a person who lacks self-control."* Without self-control, we are vulnerable to temptation and easily driven by fleeting impulses rather than enduring wisdom.

Temperance is a fruit of the Spirit (Galatians 5:23). It is not merely human willpower but Spirit-empowered restraint. It teaches us to say no to sin and yes to righteousness. It involves managing our time, words, habits, finances, and appetites according to God's principles.

A life without temperance is chaotic and unstable. But a life marked by self-control reflects the order, peace, and power of a Spirit-led believer. Living with temperance honors God and guards the destiny He has placed within us.

Teaching (Part 2):

Temperance is not about suppressing desires but bringing them under God's authority. 1 Corinthians 9:25–27 illustrates this: *"Everyone who competes in the games goes into strict training... I discipline my body and keep it under control."* Paul compares the Christian life to an athlete in training, stressing the need for discipline to reach the prize.

Self-control impacts every sphere — emotional reactions, spending habits, eating, speaking, and moral purity. Without it, our witness can be compromised, and our growth stunted. Through consistent prayer, Scripture meditation, and accountability, temperance can be strengthened.

A godly life is marked by balance, restraint, and intentional living. Temperance frees us from the tyranny of the flesh and allows the Spirit to guide our decisions. It's not restrictive — it's liberating. It positions us to walk in freedom and fulfill the purposes of God without being entangled by distractions or sin.

Reflection Questions:

1. How does the Bible describe temperance or self-control as a fruit of the Spirit?

2. In what areas of your life do you struggle most with self-control?

3. How can temperance deepen your relationship with God and strengthen your witness?

4. What practical steps can you take to grow in temperance?

5. Write a prayer asking God to cultivate deeper self-control in your daily life.

Closing Prayer:

"Father, thank You for the gift of Your Spirit that empowers me to live with temperance. Help me to exercise self-control in every area of my life — my words, my thoughts, my habits. Teach me to submit my desires to Your will and to walk in the freedom that comes from living under Your Lordship. Strengthen me daily to reflect Your discipline and love. In Jesus' name, Amen."

Verses for Meditation:

- **Proverbs 25:28** — *"Like a city whose walls are broken through is a person who lacks self-control."*
- **Galatians 5:22–23** — *"But the fruit of the Spirit is love, joy, peace... and self-control."*
- **1 Corinthians 9:25–27** — *"I discipline my body and keep it under control."*
- **Titus 2:11–12** — *"The grace of God... teaches us to say 'No' to ungodliness and worldly passions, and to live self-controlled, upright and godly lives."*
- **2 Timothy 1:7** — *"For the Spirit God gave us does not make us timid, but gives us power, love, and self-discipline."*

Key Takeaways:

- Temperance is Spirit-empowered self-control that honors God.
- A disciplined life reflects spiritual maturity and protects God's purposes for us.
- Self-control leads to freedom, stability, and a powerful witness for Christ.

Real-Life Testimony:

Elijah struggled with impulsive spending and poor time management for years. After surrendering these areas to God and seeking accountability, he began to see transformation. By practicing temperance, he paid off debts, managed his time wisely, and found greater peace. More importantly, his renewed discipline opened doors for him to serve others and mentor young men in financial stewardship and godly living. Elijah's life now demonstrates that temperance leads to lasting freedom and fruitfulness.

Chapter 29: Hope – Anchored in God's Promises

Scripture:
"The hope of the righteous will be gladness, but the expectation of the wicked will perish." – Proverbs 10:28

Introduction:
Hope is not wishful thinking—it's confident expectation in God's faithfulness. It holds us steady through grief, delay, and uncertainty.

Biblical Example:
Jeremiah spoke hope even when Jerusalem fell. He proclaimed God's mercies were new every morning. (Lamentations 3:21–23)

Reflection Questions:
- Where have I lost hope?
- What promises of God can I cling to today?
- How can I bring hope to someone else?

Practical Wisdom for Today:
- Meditate on Scriptures about God's faithfulness.
- Replace complaints with hope-filled confessions.
- Look for God's hand in the waiting.

Real-Life Story:
In a long season of unemployment, I held onto Jeremiah 29:11. Though discouraged, hope in God's plan kept me moving forward. Eventually, the breakthrough came.

Biblical Person Who Did:
Jeremiah – declared hope in the midst of despair.

Biblical Person Who Didn't:
King Saul – lost hope and turned to a medium for answers.

Key Verses to Reflect On:
- Romans 15:13
- Lamentations 3:21–23
- Hebrews 6:19

Prayer:
Lord, restore my hope. Anchor me in Your promises and help me trust Your timing. Let me be a source of hope to others. In Jesus name, Amen.

Call to Action:
Write down three promises of God and declare them aloud every morning this week.

Teaching (Part 1):

Hope is not wishful thinking; it is confident expectation based on the promises of God. Hebrews 6:19 describes hope as an anchor: *"We have this hope as an anchor for the soul, firm and secure."* Hope keeps us steady when the storms of life rage.

Biblical hope is rooted in the unchanging nature of God — His faithfulness, His goodness, and His Word. Unlike worldly hope, which is often uncertain, hope in Christ is sure and steadfast. It assures us that no matter how dark the situation, God's promises will prevail.

Hope strengthens us to endure trials, trust in unseen outcomes, and wait patiently for God's perfect timing. It lifts our eyes from present troubles and fixes them on the eternal glory that is to come. A life anchored in hope is a life filled with courage, joy, and perseverance.

Teaching (Part 2):

Romans 15:13 reminds us, *"May the God of hope fill you with all joy and peace as you trust in him."* True hope fills us with joy and peace because it is not based on circumstances but on God's character.

Hope acts as a stabilizer for the soul. It keeps us from drifting into despair or cynicism. When we cling to God's promises, we find strength to persevere and reason to rejoice, even in suffering (Romans 5:3–5). Hope gives us vision — it reminds us that this life is not all there is, and that God's best is yet to come.

A godly life is marked by unwavering hope — a hope that shines brightly in a world filled with uncertainty. Hope is not passive; it is active trust that looks forward with confidence, knowing that He who promised is faithful (Hebrews 10:23).

Reflection Questions:

1. How does biblical hope differ from the world's idea of hope?

2. In what areas of your life do you need to anchor yourself more deeply in God's promises?

3. How has hope sustained you during past trials?

4. What promises of God bring you the greatest encouragement today?

5. Write a prayer asking God to anchor your soul more firmly in His hope.

Closing Prayer:

"Father, thank You for being my unshakable hope. Anchor my soul in Your promises, and fill my heart with joy and peace as I trust in You. Teach me to fix my eyes not on what is seen but on what is eternal. Let my life overflow with the hope that only You can give, shining as a beacon to those around me. In Jesus' name, Amen."

Verses for Meditation:

- **Hebrews 6:19** — *"We have this hope as an anchor for the soul, firm and secure."*
- **Romans 15:13** — *"May the God of hope fill you with all joy and peace as you trust in him."*
- **Romans 5:3–5** — *"Suffering produces perseverance; perseverance, character; and character, hope."*
- **Hebrews 10:23** — *"Let us hold unswervingly to the hope we profess, for he who promised is faithful."*
- **Lamentations 3:21–23** — *"Yet this I call to mind and therefore I have hope: Because of the Lord's great love we are not consumed."*

Key Takeaways:

- Biblical hope is an anchor that keeps us steady through life's storms.
- Hope rests on God's unchanging promises, not on circumstances.
- A life anchored in hope reflects the joy, peace, and faithfulness of God to a watching world.

Real-Life Testimony:

Nina faced years of infertility and disappointment. Though the journey was painful, she chose to anchor her hope in God's promises rather than her circumstances. She meditated on His Word daily and clung to verses of hope. Over time, her faith deepened, her peace grew, and eventually, God blessed her with a child. Nina's story is a testament that hope anchored in God never disappoints — it strengthens us and prepares us for blessings beyond what we can imagine.

Chapter 30: Compassionate Confrontation – Speaking Truth in Love

Scripture:
"Open rebuke is better than love carefully concealed." – Proverbs 27:5

Introduction:
Godly confrontation doesn't destroy—it restores. Compassionate confrontation is truth wrapped in grace, spoken with humility for the good of others.

Biblical Example:
Nathan confronted David after his sin with Bathsheba. His words led to repentance and restoration. (2 Samuel 12:1–13)

Reflection Questions:
- Do I avoid hard conversations or enter them prayerfully?
- Am I more concerned with being right or restoring?
- How can I speak truth with grace?

Practical Wisdom for Today:
- Pray before confronting.
- Choose words and timing wisely.
- Stay gentle, not judgmental.

Real-Life Story:
A sister confronted me about an attitude I hadn't noticed. At first, I was hurt—but I knew they were right. That moment changed me. It was correction, not condemnation.

Biblical Person Who Did:
Nathan – spoke hard truth with love and purpose.

Biblical Person Who Didn't:
Eli – failed to correct his sons and lost favor with God.

Key Verses to Reflect On:
- Ephesians 4:15
- Galatians 6:1
- Proverbs 27:6

Prayer:
Lord, help me have compassion and humility. Let my words heal, not harm, and always aim for restoration. In Jesus name, Amen.

Call to Action:
If there's a hard truth you need to speak—pray, prepare, and approach with love this week.

Teaching (Part 1):

Compassionate confrontation is the courage to address issues honestly while being motivated by love. Ephesians 4:15 tells us, *"Instead, speaking the truth in love, we will grow to become in every respect the mature body of him who is the head, that is, Christ."* Truth without love can wound, but love without truth can deceive.

Healthy confrontation is essential for maintaining unity, fostering growth, and restoring relationships. It requires humility, patience, and a heart that seeks restoration, not condemnation. Speaking truth in love means choosing words that build up rather than tear down, aiming to heal rather than hurt.

Jesus modeled compassionate confrontation perfectly. He spoke directly to sin but did so with grace and a call to repentance. His goal was never to shame but to redeem. When we confront others in love, we align ourselves with His example and honor both truth and relationship.

Teaching (Part 2):

Compassionate confrontation requires wisdom. James 3:17 says, *"But the wisdom that comes from heaven is first of all pure; then peace-loving, considerate, submissive, full of mercy and good fruit, impartial and sincere."* This wisdom guides how and when we confront.

Effective confrontation starts with examining our own hearts. Are we confronting to restore or to prove a point? Galatians 6:1 instructs, *"If someone is caught in a sin, you who live by the Spirit should restore that person gently."* Gentleness is key — the goal is restoration, not humiliation.

A godly life embraces the hard work of loving confrontation because true love desires the best for others. Silence in the face of wrongdoing can be just as damaging as harsh rebuke. Compassionate confrontation, done in the Spirit of Christ, helps bring healing, growth, and stronger community bonds.

Reflection Questions:

1. Why is it important to balance truth and love in confrontation?

2. What is your natural tendency — avoiding confrontation or confronting harshly?

3. How can you prepare your heart for godly confrontation?

4. In what relationships is God calling you to speak truth in love?

5. Write a prayer asking God to help you confront others with both courage and compassion.

Closing Prayer:

"Father, teach me to speak the truth in love. Give me courage to confront when needed and wisdom to do so with gentleness and grace. Help me to seek restoration over being right and to reflect Your heart in every word I speak. May my confrontations build up and heal, always pointing others toward You. In Jesus' name, Amen."

Verses for Meditation:

- **Ephesians 4:15** — *"Speaking the truth in love, we will grow to become in every respect the mature body of him who is the head, that is, Christ."*
- **James 3:17** — *"But the wisdom that comes from heaven is first of all pure; then peace-loving, considerate, submissive, full of mercy and good fruit, impartial and sincere."*
- **Galatians 6:1** — *"Restore that person gently."*
- **Proverbs 27:5–6** — *"Better is open rebuke than hidden love. Wounds from a friend can be trusted."*
- **Matthew 18:15** — *"If your brother or sister sins, go and point out their fault, just between the two of you."*

Key Takeaways:

- Compassionate confrontation blends truth and love, aiming for restoration.
- Confronting in love requires wisdom, humility, and a heart set on reconciliation.
- When done rightly, confrontation strengthens relationships and glorifies God.

Real-Life Testimony:

Rachel noticed that a close friend was making destructive choices. Fearful of damaging the friendship, she hesitated. After much prayer, she approached her friend with love and concern, gently pointing out the danger. Her friend initially resisted but later thanked Rachel for her honesty. That conversation became a turning point, saving the friendship and helping her friend realign with God's path. Rachel's story shows that compassionate confrontation, though difficult, can bring healing and deeper trust.

Chapter 31: Finishing Well — A Life That Honors God

Introduction:

Many begin the journey of faith with passion, but few are intentional about finishing well. Life has a way of testing our devotion — disappointments, distractions, temptations, and trials can pull us off course if we're not careful. Finishing well isn't about how spectacularly you start; it's about staying faithful to God through every season and crossing the finish line with integrity, humility, and unwavering faith.

Paul, at the end of his life, summarized it beautifully:
"I have fought the good fight, I have finished the race, I have kept the faith" (2 Timothy 4:7).

Our goal is not to run quickly but to run faithfully — to live a life that honors God not just in moments of success but over a lifetime of surrender.

Biblical Example:

Paul — A Life Poured Out

Paul's journey was marked by hardship — imprisonments, shipwrecks, betrayal, persecution — yet he endured. His words near the end of his life are a testimony to steadfast faith:
"Now there is in store for me the crown of righteousness, which the Lord, the righteous Judge, will award to me on that day" (2 Timothy 4:8).

Paul's legacy wasn't built in a moment but over years of faithful service to Christ. He stayed true to his mission, finished his race, and kept the faith without wavering.

Contrast: King Saul — A Cautionary Tale

By contrast, King Saul started strong — anointed, gifted, chosen by God — but pride, disobedience, and fear led to his downfall (1 Samuel 15). Saul's life ended not with victory, but with regret and loss. His story warns us that finishing well is not automatic; it requires humility and obedience to the end.

Reflections:

- Are you living today with the finish line in mind?
- What distractions or sins threaten your endurance in the race of faith?
- How can you cultivate a heart that remains faithful over the long haul?
- Who are you becoming through the choices you make daily?

Finishing well isn't about being perfect — it's about consistently choosing to follow Christ, day after day, year after year.

Practical Wisdom:

- **Stay rooted in God's Word:** Daily Scripture reading grounds you in truth and keeps your heart aligned with God's will.
- **Maintain a posture of humility:** Recognize that finishing well requires dependence on God, not self-reliance.

- **Persevere through trials:** Trials are not detours; they are part of the journey that shapes and strengthens your faith.
- **Stay in godly community:** Surround yourself with people who encourage, challenge, and sharpen your walk with Christ.
- **Guard your heart:** Daily examine yourself before the Lord, repent quickly, and walk in obedience.

Finishing well is the sum of many small, faithful steps over a lifetime.

Real-Life Example (Who Did/Didn't Finish Well):

Who Finished Well — Billy Graham

Billy Graham preached to millions, but his greatest testimony was not his fame — it was his faithfulness. He finished his race with integrity, humility, and an unwavering commitment to the Gospel. There were no scandals, no moral failures — just a life of quiet, consistent obedience. His legacy proves that it's not about one great moment but a lifetime of small, faithful decisions.

Who Didn't Finish Well — Demas

Paul wrote with sorrow about Demas:
"For Demas, because he loved this world, has deserted me and has gone to Thessalonica" (2 Timothy 4:10).

Demas started strong as one of Paul's co-laborers but later abandoned the mission for the love of worldly things. His story is a sobering reminder that our finish matters — and that drifting often begins with small compromises.

Key Verses for Meditation:

- **2 Timothy 4:7** — *"I have fought the good fight, I have finished the race, I have kept the faith."*
- **Hebrews 12:1–2** — *"Let us run with perseverance the race marked out for us, fixing our eyes on Jesus."*
- **Galatians 6:9** — *"Let us not become weary in doing good, for at the proper time we will reap a harvest if we do not give up."*
- **1 Corinthians 9:24–25** — *"Run in such a way as to get the prize."*
- **Matthew 25:21** — *"Well done, good and faithful servant."*

Prayer:

"Lord, I want to finish well. Strengthen me to run the race with endurance. Keep me faithful when I feel weak, steadfast when I am weary, and humble when I am strong. Guard my heart against distractions and pride. Help me to keep my eyes fixed on Jesus, the Author and Finisher of my faith. Let my life glorify You until the very end. May I cross the finish line to hear You say, 'Well done, good and faithful servant.' In Jesus' name, Amen."

Call to Action:

- **Reflect:** Take time today to reflect on your journey. Are you living today in a way that honors God and prepares you to finish well?
- **Commit:** Choose one habit (prayer, Bible study, accountability) that will strengthen your faithfulness over time.

- **Encourage:** Find someone running the race and encourage them today. Finishing well is often done best in the community.

Remember: Faithfulness is not about being spectacular — it's about being steadfast. Run your race with endurance, and finish well for the glory of God.

Teaching (Part 1):

Finishing well is the crown of a life lived faithfully for God. It's not enough to begin the Christian race with passion; what truly matters is how we end. Paul's declaration in 2 Timothy 4:7 summarizes a life well lived: *"I have fought the good fight, I have finished the race, I have kept the faith."*

The Christian journey is not a sprint but a marathon. It requires endurance through trials, faithfulness during seasons of plenty and lack, and an unwavering commitment to the calling of God. Many start strong but falter when hardships arise or distractions lure them away. Finishing well is the result of a series of daily choices — to obey God, to trust Him, and to remain faithful to His Word, regardless of circumstances.

Finishing well doesn't demand perfection; it demands perseverance. It calls for humility, consistency, and a steadfast heart that, through every high and low, clings to Christ. It is a life that, until the final breath, says, *"Not my will, but Yours be done."*

Teaching (Part 2):

To finish well, we must live with the end in mind. 1 Corinthians 9:24–25 compares the Christian life to a race: *"Run in such a way as to get the prize. Everyone who competes in the games goes into strict training."* Spiritual endurance, like physical endurance, requires discipline and intentionality.

Daily habits fuel a life that finishes well — prayer, Scripture study, community with other believers, serving, and worshiping. These disciplines are the training grounds for perseverance.

Galatians 6:9 reminds us: *"Let us not become weary in doing good, for at the proper time we will reap a harvest if we do not give up."* Weariness is real, but hope fuels endurance. God promises a harvest for those who stay faithful. And the greatest reward is not earthly accolades, but hearing the Savior say, *"Well done, good and faithful servant"* (Matthew 25:21).

Finishing well also means leaving a legacy. It is passing on faith, love, and godly wisdom to the next generation. It is living a life that continues to bear fruit long after we are gone. A godly life that finishes well reflects the faithfulness of God and points others to His grace.

Reflection Questions:

1. What does "finishing well" mean to you personally in your journey of faith?

2. Are there areas in your life where complacency or distraction have threatened your endurance?

3. What daily disciplines can help you stay focused on running your race well?

4. Who in your life has modeled finishing well, and what can you learn from their example?

5. Write a prayer asking God for strength and focus to finish the race of faith well.

Closing Prayer:

"Father, thank You for calling me to run the race of faith. Strengthen me to endure every trial and temptation that comes my way. Help me to live with the end in mind, to remain faithful, and to glorify You in every season. Keep me humble, diligent, and dependent on Your grace. May I finish well and hear the words, 'Well done, good and faithful servant.' In Jesus' name, Amen."

Verses for Meditation:

- **2 Timothy 4:7** — *"I have fought the good fight, I have finished the race, I have kept the faith."*
- **Hebrews 12:1–2** — *"Let us run with perseverance the race marked out for us, fixing our eyes on Jesus."*
- **Galatians 6:9** — *"Let us not become weary in doing good, for at the proper time we will reap a harvest if we do not give up."*
- **1 Corinthians 9:24–25** — *"Run in such a way as to get the prize."*
- **Matthew 25:21** — *"Well done, good and faithful servant."*

Key Takeaways:

- Finishing well is the result of daily faithfulness, endurance, and focus on Christ.
- A life that finishes well reflects God's grace and leaves a legacy of faith for others.
- The greatest reward is not worldly recognition but hearing God's commendation: *"Well done."*

Real-Life Testimony:

Pastor James served his church faithfully for over five decades. Though faced with personal loss, illness, and seasons of discouragement, he never wavered in his devotion to God. Even in his final days, he encouraged others, prayed earnestly, and shared the Gospel. At his memorial, countless lives testified to the impact of his faithful witness. Pastor James' life embodied finishing well — not in fame or fortune, but in steadfast love for God and people.

Conclusion: A Life Well-Lived in Godliness

As we conclude this journey through Proverbs and the walk of godliness, remember godliness is not a destination, but a daily devotion. It is the consistent, humble pursuit of a heart fully aligned with God's will.

Godliness touches every part of our lives, our thoughts, actions, relationships, and service. It transforms how we love, forgive, endure, and hope. Through diligence in the Word and surrender to the Holy Spirit, you are being shaped into the image of Christ day by day.

Let these truths settle deep in your soul:

- Godliness is not perfection, it's progression.
- Wisdom is not information, it's transformation.
- Walking with God requires humility, patience, and trust.

Keep your heart soft before the Lord. Seek Him first. Trust Him always. And remember, the journey to godliness is not walked alone. God is with you—guiding, empowering, and perfecting all that concerns you.

May your life be a living testimony to the goodness and glory of God.

Reflection Prayer

Heavenly Father,

Thank You for walking with me through this journey of godliness. I surrender my heart, my will, and my plans to You. Teach me daily to seek Your wisdom, to love others as You have loved me, and to walk humbly in Your ways. Strengthen me when I grow weary, and remind me that Your grace is sufficient for every step. May my life bring glory to Your name and reflect Your character to all I encounter.
In Jesus name, Amen.

About the Author

Risa Stegall is the founder of Shepherd's Word Publishing, a ministry birthed from a deep desire to honor God through writing and teaching His Word. Guided by the Holy Spirit, Risa blends biblical truth with real-life application to help others live purposefully and powerfully in Christ. Her work is rooted in prayer, grounded in Scripture, and centered on glorifying God in all things.

Connect with Risa and discover more resources at:
Shepherd's Word Publishing:
shepherdsword@shepherdswordpublishing.com

More Books by Risa Stegall

- The Choice That Changed Everything: Walking in Wisdom in a World of Folly

- Walking in Wisdom: 31-Day Declarations
  (A Companion to The Choice That Changed Everything) *

- Blessings from Above: A Daily Family Prayer Guide

- Coming Soon: Resilient Faith: Christ and His Faithful Overcoming Life's Hardships

- And more to come from Shepherd's Word Publishing!

Connect with Risa

Thank you for reading Walking in Godliness. I would love to stay connected with you!

For updates, devotionals, and new releases:

Email: shepherdsword@shepherdswordpublishing.com

May God bless you richly as you continue to walk in wisdom and godliness.